Wiccecræft

Shamanic Magic
from
The Dark Ages

by
Sinead Spearing

GREEN
MAGIC

Green Magic
5 Stathe Cottages
Stathe
Somerset
TA7 0JL
England
www.greenmagicpublishing.com
info@greenmagicpublishing.com

Typeset by Green Man Books, Dorchester
greenmangallery@lineone.net

ISBN 978-0-9561886-2-5

GREEN MAGIC

This book is dedicated to Jan, my angel
and Cassie my muse.

I acknowledge and thank the Anglo-Saxon scholar Stephen Pollington for kindly permitting me to use his own translations of the Lacnunga, Bald's Leechbook and the Old English Herbarium. I would also like to thank Brian Bates for his books on the subject of 'wyrd' which drew my attention to the stories of King Edwin and Thorbiorg. My heartfelt thanks also go to my dear husband for his tireless support and inspiration without which this book could not have been written, and my sister, friend and poet Sian Thomas for her words of wisdom and encouragement. Also to Granddad for setting me on the right path.

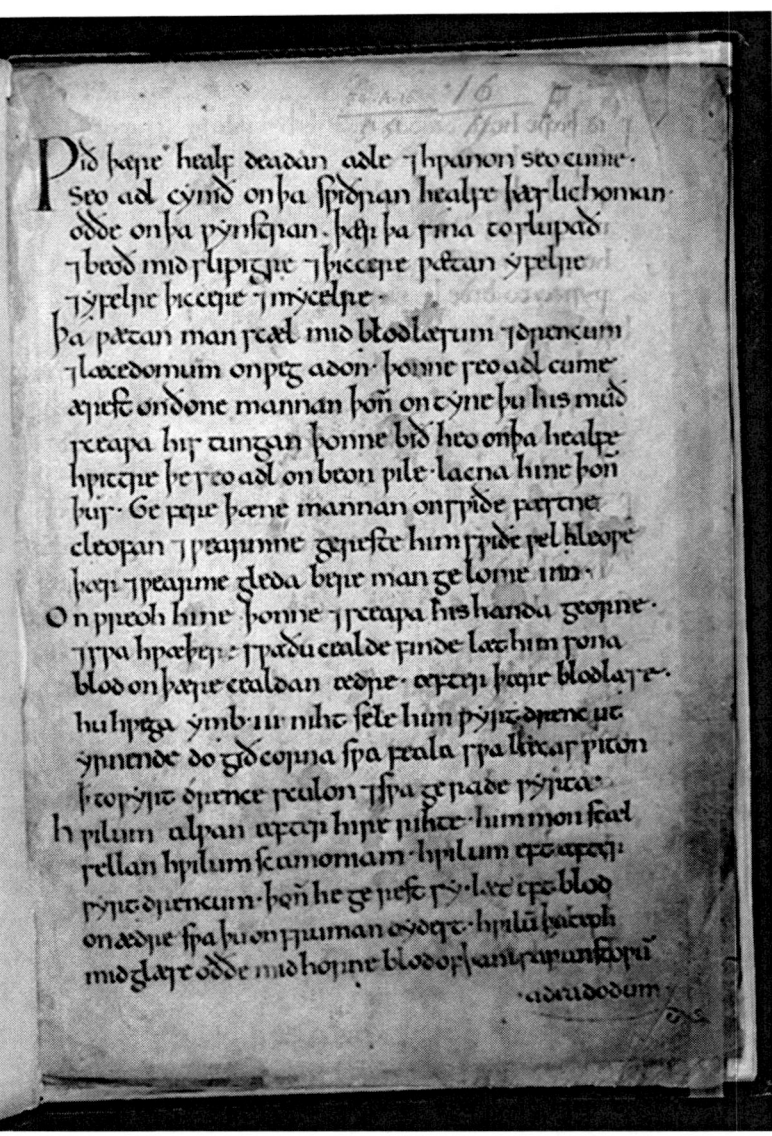

A page from Bald's Leechbook Royal M.S 12. D.xvii. 9th century.

IV

CONTENTS

INTRODUCTION

The old veiled one, Ceridwen, Cailleach, Morrighan once prophesied of a future world where...

> *"I shall not see a world that will be dear to me.*
> *Summer without flowers,*
> *Kine will be without milk,*
> *Women without modesty,*
> *Men without valour,*
> *Captures without a King...*
> *Woods without mast,*
> *Sea without produce*
> *Wrong judgements of old men...*
> *An evil time!"*

One cannot help but wonder whether such a world is soon to be our own. A world so lost it is no longer dear to the mother who bore it, a mother with the power however, to bring about its death in order to birth it again renewed. If ever there was a time to heed her anguished cry of mourning it is now, and fortunately, increasing numbers of us are beginning to listen to her call. We are sensing the need for a re-connection with Mother Nature, to seek something more than that which appears before us as modern life. I hear the call myself and have listened at length to the lament of others who equally yearn for greater meaning in life and a healthier respect and relationship with our natural world. It is this call which has inspired me to explore the Craft before its modern incarnations to discover the ancient ways and practices which aided our ancestors in their experience of a magical world. This book is for Witches, Wiccans and non-witches alike who hear the call to an older path when we still encountered and experienced magic in the mundane.

This book emerges from a life time of work, exploration and celebration. As a student and practitioner of various magical paths since childhood I have had the great privilege to work with many Witches, Magicians and spiritual souls from a variety of traditions, always learning, always listening, and over the years I have become ever aware of that unrelenting yet often muffled cry for a more meaningful, rich and essential experience of the magical crafts and life in general. We seem to have an instinct, a peculiar 'knowing' that within our world dominated by the acquisition of 'things' and the de-valuation of nature, that something of humanity has been lost.

A 'new age' has erupted in a reactionary urge to address this in-balance which threatens to reduce humanity to a soulless state within a soulless world. We have Paganism, Wicca, Feminist Witchcraft, Green Witchcraft, Modern Druidry and many more movements pushing forward this new impulse for a re-evaluation of our relationship with the Universe, the Earth and each other. Unfortunately however, within this reactionary stance, well intended though it certainly is, something of the ancient Craft is also lost.

It is my aim to uncover a forgotten wisdom, a knowledge of which our ancestors in Northern Europe lived and breathed and once un-earthed, I then present rituals, meditations and exercises which will show modern seekers how to have an experience of this ancient way of knowing and living. Although much exploration has been afforded magic in the classical era and more recently, anthropologists have looked to indigenous aboriginal cultures too, our own ancestors of Northern Europe and particularly England have been largely forgotten, hidden in the apparent 'dark ages' of myth and legend.

However, ancient texts of the period although often obscure, do survive and they shed light on a period of history in England which is far from dark and barbarous. England was, and still is a 'coming together' of many different peoples, the Celtic, Germanic, Norse and more. It is commonly thought therefore that a magical or spiritual identity for England is not worth pursuing, but as more evidence comes to light through historic delving, certain common themes emerge which point to a rich indigenous and shamanic heritage which we may explore and embrace to enhance our modern world if we so chose.

The dark ages of Anglo-Saxon England are now being illuminated and as they shine forth we may begin to remember an old way of being. We may already feel it in our bones, smell it on the breeze on a warm summer's evening, encounter it within an embrace or taste it on the lips of a lover. This book combines this instinctive knowing with original insight, celebrating the Craft of the old way which runs deep in our blood, pulsing through veins and visiting in the night as ancient dreams awakening the unconscious from its slumber. The darkness of the unconscious mind then finds it is no longer imprisoned. Imagination, fantasy, magic, wonder, psychic abilities and prophetic dreams are no longer the abnormalities in a hostile world, they are our freedom, they are our truth and will re-enchant our lives. This book points the way for such discovery and remembering.

The term 'shamanism' once referred solely to the indigenous

magical figures of ancient Siberian tribes peoples. However, with increasing anthropological investigations this term has expanded to refer to almost any indigenous magical and spiritual cultural practice and therefore, the ancient Craft magic of England and Northern Europe nestles snugly into this useful category. Witches, Seers, Druids and Sorcerers all fit within this term and the boundaries of their claims to our magical heritage is fluid. My focus remains however, upon exploring the ancient shamanic origins specific to modern witchcraft which was re-formed in the mid-twentieth century by the late great Gerald Gardner. To this end I will be delving into many magical texts. Some are from the modern and medieval eras but mostly I take inspiration from the few surviving texts of dark ages England.

Written in Old English, the magical texts which form my main source material are the Anglo-Saxon medico-magical manuscripts currently held in The British Library. There are a number of these Old English works surviving in the collections known as Harley 585 and Royal M.S 12 although the Lacnunga manuscript and Bald's Leechbooks, particularly number three, are the focus and inspiration for this book. The Lacnunga, Bald's Leechbook and further texts such as the Old English Herbarium are generally thought to have been written down between 900-1000.A.D from earlier sources. Some of these sources are classical having been translated from Latin into Old English although other sources, particularly those of Leechbook number three (Book III) are almost pure English except for the odd nugget of Old Irish which only serves to confirm its authenticity as perhaps the only surviving medico-magical text exclusively from these British Isles.

The Lacnunga manuscript, although certainly containing Mediterranean influences nonetheless combines these with some very traditional English folk remedies. It is an unsophisticated text, badly organised with a myriad of copying mistakes and inconsistencies causing many scholars to ignore its value. It was probably compiled as a simple personal resource. Its value for those with magical understanding however, is vast.

In contrast, Bald's Leechbook Book III is well organised and displayed with few, if any, classical appropriations leading some to speculate it to have been commissioned by Alfred the Great or more probably by one of his medical advisors. There is a wealth of traditional Anglo-Saxon magic preserved here as well as the names and methods of collection, application and ritualistic significance of native British herbs. Both The Lacnunga and Leechbook afford us the rare and unique opportunity to re-connect with the wise healers and witches of our Anglo-Saxon past.

These amazing and long forgotten manuscripts are the inspiration for my work and I situate them within a larger indigenous context of traditional shamanic witchcraft spanning England and Northern Europe from the pre-historic past through to the present day. In the Old English (OE) language the term for witch was wicce pronounced as '*witche*' as the double 'c' was sounded as 'ch'. The familiar term Wicca is actually the masculine and later version of the original feminine wicce, and it is this original term that I shall use throughout the book to describe our early shamanic brothers and sisters of the Craft.

Each chapter focuses upon a particular aspect of the ancient shamanic Craft of Anglo-Saxon England such as healing, divination and magic and offers specifically designed meditations, rituals and exercises aimed to develop a real experience of ancient Craft practices. Central to these practices however, was a way of experiencing the world which was very different to our own and it is this subtle difference in perception which will be explored within the first chapter.

The first chapter is concerned with a process of re-orientation of our every-day awareness towards a shamanic magical consciousness. It aims to expose the living reality of the Otherworld, a realm of powerful forces recognised by our ancestors as spirits and entities which were every bit as real and tangible as beings within our own world. Although distinct, this Otherworld was intimately connected in relationship and causality with our own and for those skilful enough to work within its energies and direct its forces, the Otherworld became a source of powerful knowledge which could affect changes in our current reality. This Otherworld was composed of many realms some close to us and others further away. Our own physical world is in the middle and was known therefore as middle earth (or '*middengeard*' in Old English). This cosmological and essentially shamanic view is a central theme to the book and revisits within every chapter.

Today, although many witches work with the power of the Otherworld, we have lost the immediacy of our relationship with it and thus the full potential of its gifts. We are assuaged of a myriad of rationalist assumptions which are difficult if not impossible to overcome and so this book aims not to strip away our modern consciousness but to enhance it with a re-membering of the ancient living and experiential nature of the Craft. To this end, the first chapter concludes by suggesting an exercise to develop a powerful technique of conscious awareness which the famous psychologist C.G. Jung termed the alchemical imagination.

In reality, the alchemical imagination is itself an ancient resource, once taken for granted but in our modern world forgotten and subordinated in the Western rise of intellectualism and reason which argued imagination to be at best mere illusion and at worst, the work of the devil! By experiencing and using the alchemical imagination however, we can synthesise our modern mind with our ancient past to re-capture a truly magical consciousness.

The second chapter explores the wicce's direct relationship with herbs and plants. I present within this chapter a rare resource of ancient spells and remedies from the ancient manuscripts. These are provided in Old English as they appear in the texts along with Modern English translations presented here by kind permission of the Anglo-Saxon scholar Stephen Pollington. I include Old English many times throughout the book to give the reader an opportunity to read and even speak this magically lilting sing-song language which inspired Tolkien's 'Elvish' in The Lord of The Rings, to this end I include a basic guide to pronunciation as an appendix. At the end of the chapter is a further meditation activity to help develop the ancient ability to 'compel' herbs to reveal their powers to us.

Chapter three looks into the mysterious skill of direct divination. Divination is not just an interpretative action using runes or the positions of stars although our wicce ancestors certainly utilised such skills in abundance. So much has been written of interpretative divination however, that I focus specifically upon the more ineffable skill of inspirational, revelatory and ecstatic immersion into the Otherworld from which all knowledge flows regardless of the constructs of past, present and future. The skilled wicce would often immerse themselves directly into this flowing energy and emerge transformed with answers to questions regarding any type of query including the prediction of future events. It is difficult to develop such a skill and very little has ever been written regarding it yet I suggest a ritual to begin the process. Chapter four which explores shapeshifting continues in similar style.

Chapter five is completely different however, and concerns the actual practices, rituals, and initiations of traditional shamanic witchcraft today. I did not wish to simply list these practices as an alternative book of shadows but to bring them alive in the spirit of the oral and experiential tradition from which they emerge. To achieve a more animated and experiential quality to this important section I have chosen to tell the story of a new witch approaching the shamanic craft of the wicce for the first time. From her first initiation into the tribe of Andredswold and her experience of its main rites to her observations of the teachings and structures of the tribe itself, this pseudo-fictional diary traces the journey of the new traveller.

It is my aim within these pages to present the indigenous shamanic witchcraft of our ancestors in a way which awakens yet retains the spirit of the old ways (*fyrn sidu* in OE), where teaching and learning occurred within the lived experience of daily life, and story-telling preserved these wisdoms for generations. The result is a newly empowered type of ancient witchcraft which emerges from the journey we will have taken through this book.

It is not my intention to romanticise the past, there is no doubt that early and mediaeval England could be a very harsh place to live and few would truly wish to literally go back in time. However, we may expand our awareness by remembering how our ancient brothers and sisters of the Craft viewed their world to see what we can learn from them to benefit and enrich our modern lives, societies and relationships.

1. THE OTHERWORLD AND THE ALCHEMICAL IMAGINATION

Central to the magical practices and magical lives of our ancestors was the mysterious realm known as the Otherworld. It was a place inhabited by mythic beings such as elves, dwarves and many types of daemon. It was also home to the spirits of the dead but most importantly, it was experienced by our ancestors as being every bit as real as our normal mundane physical reality.

The powerful energies which flow from the Otherworld into our own spin like a web through our meagre reality, offering us a glimpse at something greater than our world of 'things'. Our ancestors felt this flowing energy. A feeling in the bones, the prickling of hair on the nape of the neck, small sympathetic 'knowings' reminding them that powers were at work beyond the scope of their human eyes, which had consequences for every action they were to take in their world. Even today we intuitively sense this parallel dimension which can at times seem so very close, just a heartbeat away yet ultimately elusive and ineffable. We may chance upon it in dreams or meditations or perhaps in a moment of reverie whilst watching a beautiful sunset, but such encounters are rare and fleeting. For the wicce however, the Otherworld offered more than just brief glimpses of power, they were able to harness and use the energy from this elusive realm to work magic and healing in this physical reality.

The wicce used rituals as structural support for their journeys and communications with beings and entities from the Otherworld. Ritual would aid a subtle shift in consciousness whilst framing the intent of the magic to be performed, so both worlds could be in no doubt regarding the desired outcome. Offerings would be made to Otherworldly beings encouraging their participation before magical processes would be performed to ensure the required changes in this reality would indeed occur.

A mixture of invocation and symbolic sympathetic magic was commonly employed and combined with a powerful use of imagination directed towards the intended goal. Today we have lost much of our ability to recognise this Otherworld as truly real, often believing that we can only connect with it within the confines of a circle where we feel safe to enter alternative states of consciousness which serve to help us remember who we really are. This belief is false. Our ancestors understood that the magical Otherworld is here right now, and we can live it in every moment in an enchanted reality.

We need therefore, to remember and truly re-experience this Otherworldly reality if we are to recover a meaningful and powerful relationship with the Craft and life in general. To achieve this end it is necessary for us to change more than just our ritualistic habits. We need to re-immerse ourselves within a world view which animates our relationship with both the natural world and the Otherworld of magical beings, energies and the divine. Our ancestors were possessed of a perspective on life and the universe very different to our own, where no disconnection from nature and the spirits which guarded it existed. The Otherworld was a reality for all people not just the wicce, although it was the wicce who could work and direct its energies to affect the material realm.

Life for our ancestors was thus animated and full of meaning. The flight patterns of certain birds may be portentous of a good harvest or the appearance of a large crow may tell of ill fortune ahead. Everything was interconnected in a wide web of knowledge and relationship weaving through everything that existed, exists and will exist in the future. There was no fragmentation or alienation. Although most modern witches and magic workers instinctively 'know' this to be true, it is a rare witch indeed who really has an authentic and consistent living experience of this ancient way of being. We seem to 'know' one thing yet experience another and subsequently our craft-working becomes diminished from its full potential. This is unsurprising given our post-modern assumptions regarding the authenticity of intuition, imagination and magic. We have been brain washed since the cradle to be dismissive of that which we cannot see immediately before our eyes. The unconscious, the mad, psychic experience and synchronicities, anything not snugly accommodated by modern empirical science is to be feared and subordinated in preference to reason and rationality.

However, some chinks of light are finding their way into the minds of our modern thinkers and a leading voice in the call for a greater understanding of the Otherworld has been the voice of the French mystical philosopher Henry Corbin. Corbin's life work was centred upon the mysticism of the East yet his main findings focus upon the commonality of the Otherworld.

Corbin's research demonstrates that the Otherworld was not unique to the wicce in England but existed also for the Shamans of Siberia, the Aborigines of Australia, the ancient Egyptians, the Sufism of the East and many more indigenous cultures who described just such a world. The Otherworld is therefore a common and uniting theme within all magical and spiritual systems and beliefs. It is an enduring spiritual principle, although it may have been called by different names and conceptualised in different ways depending upon cultural differences through time.

Corbin terms the Otherworld the *Mundus Imaginalis* to indicate the 'imaginal' or symbolic quality of the realm and it is our imagination he argues, which enables us to relate to the Otherworld and harness its wisdom and energy. He is not talking about imagination as a function of cognition such as our ability to process images in our minds-eye, problem-solve or even our ability to visualise or paint pictures. He is talking about a role of imagination far beyond what any of us ever encounter in our normal lives, and I will explain and develop this point further when we come to the meditation exercise at the end of this chapter.

For Corbin, the Otherworld is a pre-condition of our own world, meaning that our world would not exist without it. The Otherworld thus encompasses our reality rather than being situated by it. He explains this difficult concept by using the following analogy. Although we commonly consider our spirit to be situated within our body or brain during its incarnation, an assumption forced upon us by Descartes' separation of the mind from the body (and the natural world), the converse is actually true. The body is encompassed by the spirit. Furthermore, imagination, which has the ability to connect with and move between the two worlds, encompasses our psychological and cognitive functions. We are therefore embraced and held by a world of magic which appears to us in visions, dreams and symbols yet it is a world to which we have become increasingly blind and mute.

We have been led to believe that magic is false, and that we are powerless 'fallen' beings who have been cast out of a utopian paradise due to our inherent evilness. Even though we may eschew such a notion it is embedded deeply within our modern psyche pulling our eyes firmly shut. But let us sing from the tree tops and dance from the woodlands that we are not to be limited. We are part of a magnificent universe far greater and more powerful than the small categories and boxes in which modern science and religions would bind us. Let us re-orientate our reality and remember the potential of who we are and how great we can be. Our greatest teachers have always taught that the Kingdom of God is here right now, which suggests that our intimacy and immediacy with the Otherworld is a consistent truth. We do not need to go anywhere, just alter our awareness and open our eyes.

I suggest therefore, that we can recover the wisdom of the Otherworld within our modern existence, to re-enchant humanity. We must begin however, by finding our way to the realm of magic aided by imagination. The imagination is our portal which marks the veil between the two worlds, where the energies flow constantly back and forth, and we must dip our toes into this flowing watery meeting point.

The importance of this flowing energy and the wicce who were gifted with seeing and interpreting it, can be demonstrated in the following famous historic account of King Edwin's conversion, and the killing of the prophesising crow. The Anglo-Saxon Chronicles state that King Edwin, ruler of Northumbria in the early seventh century converted to Christianity in A.D.601 being baptised by Bishop Paulinus. Having forsaken Odin and the old Gods, Edwin had also relieved his wicce advisors of their posts. The wicce had been responsible for guiding the King by interpreting omens and providing healing and prophecy to strengthen the Kingdom.

One Sunday morning as King Edwin was walking to Church accompanied by his new Christian guides and advisors, the group came to an abrupt halt due to the sudden appearance of a large black crow which, totally without fear despite the large entourage of humans, began to sing with great authority. King Edwin was terror struck; recognising this to be an important omen yet being without any wicce with their wisdom to interpret it, the King was ignorant of its full meaning. The monks, seeing this as a pagan challenge to their new God's authority demanded the bird shot with an arrow. They delivered the crow to the King its death as evidence, so they presumed, to the superiority and power of the Christian God over the pagan Gods which had sent the evil bird.

The monks were wrong. Crows were considered to be messengers from the Otherworld, and Odin himself had two crows that would fly the land and report to him with their findings. What the monks could not understand was that the bird was intended to die anyway. It had emerged directly from the Otherworld, sent by spirits and the divine energies to deliver an important message to the King. After the message had been delivered the bird would have returned to the Otherworld by way of its death. Without the wicce, gifted with a magical consciousness which could see the subtle movement of energies between the two worlds, the bird's message remained un-interpreted. The acceptance by the King of a Christianised consciousness left him isolated from the Otherworld, unable to read its signs and be guided by its wisdom. The monks who celebrated the bird's death as a sign from their God that pagan values had been defeated, were blind to the reality of what had just happened and within a short time of this event, the King was dead.

Although King Edwin had recognised the Crow to be a messenger from the Otherworld, he did not possess the skill to interpret the omen himself. The wicce, our brothers and sisters of old were attuned to the flowing between the worlds, and skilful in translating the symbols and directing the energy when required. We have lost control and knowledge of this imaginal ability, yet as the magical scholar Lévy-Bruhl describes:

'between outer tangible reality and inner states of mind, or between

body and a fuzzy conglomerate of mind, psyche and spirit. We have lost the third, middle position which (is) the place of the soul: a world of imagination, passion, fantasy.... that is neither physical and material on the one hand, nor spiritual and abstract on the other, yet bound to them both.'

(La Mentalité primitive, 1947)

This strange 'middle position' of imagination must be restored within our modern consciousness. We are so accustomed however, to a dualistic world which appears in black and white terms, good/bad, rich/poor, wrong/right, above/below etc that to embrace a multiplicity of reality is uncomfortable. Furthermore, we are often encouraged by new-age thinkers, scientists and modern philosophers that this duality must be collapsed into a singularity, a unifying principle which is ultimate reality and the goal of our existence. However, as will become clearer as this book continues, singularity is paradoxically, multiple. The one God is many, and the ultimate truth is not an end goal to be attained but rather, a journey to be experienced moment to moment.

Reconnecting the two worlds, developing the alchemical imagination

The Jungian psychoanalyst Dr Marie-Louise von Franz wrote in her book 'The Alchemical Active Imagination' that the Otherworld is:

'the plane on which active imagination takes control. With the inner nucleus of consciousness you stay in the middle place.... you stay within your active imagination, so to speak, and you have the feeling that this is where your life process goes on.'

Working with the active (or alchemical in Jungian terms) imagination in order to re-connect with the Otherworld requires a shift of consciousness combined with an expansion of awareness, and no other figure has devised more ways to achieve this than

7

C. G. Jung.

Jung came from a spiritual family. His Mother was fascinated with the occult, and the young Jung experienced many powerful dreams where he conversed with spirit entities as well as his own ancestors. Jung's concept of the collective unconscious is very similar to that of the wicce's Otherworld, except that Jung mapped out the dominant energies and impulses of the realm as they appear to us as archetypes. This enabled a conceptual understanding of the Otherworld however, although Jung personally believed the Otherworld to be ontologically real, his development of psychoanalysis implied it to be nothing more than the working of the unconscious mind and therefore, the Otherworld became viewed as simply being part of our internal psychological processes. A deeper reading of Jung's work demonstrates this common view to be misguided.

Imagination is a vast and ultimately mysterious power. The Swiss physician and mystic Paracelsus wrote:

'*It is necessary that you should know what can be accomplished by a strong imagination. It is the principle of all magical action... And this imagination is such that it penetrates and ascends into the superior heaven, and passes from star to star.*'

Imagination thus encompasses both this and the Otherworld, whilst functioning equally as the energy which unites them. It is the web that connects everything together and it is the foundation upon which, wisdom is formed.

It often appears to our perception as if there are different levels of imagination. Firstly we have a cognitive imagination which associates images and problem-solves. Secondly we have an egoic form of phantasy which indulges the wants and desires of the bound ego. Thirdly there is the more creative form of imagination utilised in the arts, path-workings and the like and finally, we have the alchemical imagination, the function of our higher magical consciousness. These levels do not describe distinct categories, as imagination is a constant power which different human functions utilise in different ways. The ego can employ it to deceive and limit us if we remain unaware of its desires. This is because imagination is morally neutral, neither good nor bad. Imagination pre-exists our quaint efforts to categorise and evaluate our experiences.

The alchemical imagination is currently the highest functional experience of imaginative work we seem able to attain. Gaining an experience however, can take time and effort and at first it can feel as if we have been pushed out to sea on a boat with no oars or sail, waiting for some sign that we are at least going in the right direction. The following exercise is designed to awaken an initial experience of what it feels like to encounter the reality of the imaginal realm of the Otherworld. It will not necessarily happen overnight, if only it would! I have developed the exercise from an old alchemical manuscript called *The Book of Lambspring (De Lapide Philosophico Libellus),* which contains the most beautiful and mysterious alchemical symbolic emblems. Alchemists would utilise the emblems to access the Otherworld through a powerful engagement of alchemical imagination.

Awakening to an experience of the alchemical imagination

You will need a tarot card or an image of, the High Priestess. This card more than any other, embodies within its symbolism the veil that exists between this and the Otherworld. You do not require a comprehensive knowledge of this trump card's meaning indeed; no knowledge is required at all. The idea is not to bring a pre-conceived interpretation to the image but instead, to allow the symbols to speak to you from the Otherworld.

Begin by finding a quiet time when you are unlikely to be disturbed, have a pen and paper handy and then relax in whatever way you wish. You may choose to meditate upon your breathing, candle gaze or chant, just allow the material world to become less important and let the thinking mind drift. When you feel relaxed gently turn your eyes to the High Priestess. Observe the card and its symbols dispassionately, do not attempt to interpret the images, just become aware of the shapes and forms washing over you. When you feel the time is right, close your eyes and allow the images to form in your mind's-eye. It doesn't matter if the image is not exactly the same as the card, in fact it may become very different. Watch the scene begin to take shape in your mind in whatever way seems right.

The next step is to begin by gently flexing and using your alchemical imagination, and this step can take some practice before it fully engages. Until this point you have utilised your imagination which processes and combines images for the mind, and now it is time to let go the reins and allow imagination to truly create a new experience. If you can, step into the scene that you created in your mind's-eye and relax again, try not to let the thinking mind dominate too much. Look around you and notice the colours, sounds and smells of the scene. Feel the air temperature, notice the time of the day and simply experience the situation as fully as possible.

However, this is not a path-working or guided meditation and the next step is completely and utterly in your hands. You need to allow whatever needs to happen, happen. You may feel an impulse to go towards the High Priestess, if indeed she is still there. You may be approached by someone totally different, or perhaps an animal guide will come forward and beckon you to follow. It is okay to enter into dialogue with figures you meet and ask them questions, or you may feel drawn to simply sit within the countryside, still, contemplative, open. Whatever occurs, do not force it and try not to evaluate or question its validity. When you feel it's time to return then just come back, remember you have not really *been* anywhere at all.

This type of imaginative work does not always come easily. The Otherworld is not a cognitive realm and with our minds so accustomed to the relentless urge to interpret and evaluate absolutely everything, it is difficult to trust our imagination to journey authentically. Furthermore, there is a difference between active alchemical imagination and the fantasies of the egoic mind. As previously mentioned, imagination is employed by the ego just as readily as it is employed by mind and spirit. Do not be too concerned however; as you practise this exercise and perhaps move on to other tarot cards or your own alchemical images you will gradually be able to tell the difference. Generally, egoic employment of imagination may leave you with an initial feeling of satisfaction which soon fades to reveal a de-energised, slightly depressive or even an anxious state, without any new knowledge or perspectives on life. An authentic engagement of the alchemical imagination which touches the Otherworld will feel energising, uplifting, meaningful and life changing. As the Jungian theorist Jeffrey Raff explains:

'By seeking the meaning of life events [through the alchemical imagination], the ego escapes from the illusory world of fantasy that only sees concrete reality and appearances. A conflict with a boss, a car accident, a headache....- all of these events- may be perceived with the eyes of the imagination. Such a perspective frees one from the sense of being trapped in the situation, and permits one to seek the meaning related to it. Working with meaning opens up possibilities that were hidden before.'

(Jung and the Alchemical Imagination, 2000)

In conclusion, the Otherworld is very real. It permeates and embraces us in every way imaginable. It holds our life and brings meaning to our experiences. Nothing need remain unknown or hidden if we trust, accept and become proficient in working with this powerful realm. The Otherworld is where creative energy springs forth unbounded by human attempts to limit and control it. It is imaginal in nature and requires us to use a highly developed form of alchemical imagination to swim its waters. However, witches of old were able to interpret its signs and direct its energies to provide healing and transformations within the material world, and with this magical realm in mind and our relationship with it deepening, we can gain a far greater understanding and a more powerful experience, of witchcraft.

F

2. ANCIENT HEALING

Writing in the early sixteenth century, Paracelsus explained that '*He who is born in imagination finds out the latent forces of Nature, [and] He who imagines compels herbs to put forth their hidden nature.*' Although greatly respected within the medical establishment Paracelsus retained a marked interest in the old path of healing, which recognised that we live within an animated and interconnected reality. He was fascinated by alchemy and the occult, always pursuing the spiritual facet of medicine and healing whenever convention allowed. His comment above implies an understanding that healers require to be reborn or rather, initiated into the mysteries of the Otherworld through a cultivation of the alchemical imagination, which would enable the healer to perceive the hidden nature of herbs.

Hundreds of years ago in Britain however, before the time of Paracelsus, had I been ill I would have had cause to visit the local wicce. Let us say I had an acute attack of psoriasis and although I would probably have felt some apprehension, fearful of what I may be asked to endure, the wicce would have been considered the only person capable of relieving my troublesome symptoms.

Upon my arrival, as an ancient text describes, I would have told of my ailment and then watched as the wicce prepared my medicine.

The wicce may have taken *'goose-fat, and the lower part of elecampane and viper's bugloss, bishop's wort, and cleavers.'* Then the wicce would have *'pound the four herbs together well, squeeze them out, and add a spoonful of soap. Add a little oil, then mix it thoroughly.'* After dispensing the ointment into a small leather pouch, I would have left with the instructions to *'lather it on at night. Scratch the neck after sunset, and gently pour the blood into running water, spit three times upon it and say, "Take this disease and depart with it." Go back to the house by an open road, and go in silence.'*

If I suffered from psoriasis today I would visit my local doctor in the small village where I live in England. She may also prescribe some sort of topical ointment such as coal tar paste or calcipotriol, or even a combination of different creams with complimentary active agents. These modern creams have various properties. For example, they act to moisturise the skin similarly to goose-fat, and calm the inflamed skin like the herb 'cleavers'. It is of course unlikely that my doctor would direct me to pour blood from my skin into running water and spit three times, but it is quite probable I would be asked to adopt some small ritual observance such applying the ointment at a certain time of day for a particular period of time.

The two experiences, ancient and modern, are not so terribly distinct indicating that the boundaries between magic and medicine were, and arguably still are, flexible. Even elements of the magical and ritualistic healing practices of the wicce which have been dismissed for centuries as mere superstition, are closer to our modern conception of disease then we have been led to believe.

Although scholars and physicians acknowledge the benefit of certain herbal concoctions, they have dismissed the validity of the more magical aspects of healing due to what they have interpreted as spurious and ignorant ancient beliefs. For example, the wicce and our ancestors believed that illnesses were caused by attacks from entities sent from the Otherworld. Of particular concern was the mischievous behaviour of elves who would fire their arrows into people, bringing about an illness which the wicce called 'elf-shot'. The arrows were full of elven energy and magic which would invade the victim and take over their bodies, diminishing health. To the modern mind such beliefs may certainly appear quaint and superstitious yet the wicce were not the only peoples to believe that elven arrows caused disease.

The Amazonian Shuar tribes also believe that much disease is caused by little arrows fired from the spirits of the Otherworld. These arrows called *tsentsak* carry the energy of the malevolent spirit to infect the victim, much akin to a poisoned dart. To extract the venom, the Shuar shaman would perform rituals to transfer the energy from the arrows into themselves and then out again into a flowing stream to be purified of the malicious intent. Chanting, incantations and mind altering plants would be utilised to pull the bad energy from the victim and the Shaman would often be seen to vomit the arrows out into water to affect the cure.

Although the Shuar were thousands of miles away from the wicce the similarity of belief here is uncanny. Many people today argue that this is because there was far more contact between ancient peoples than we are prepared to accept and perhaps beliefs were shared. Although I tend to believe in the theory of early cross fertilisation, the shamanic heritage shared by almost every indigenous culture on the planet seems more complex and profound than a sharing of belief. The commonality was not of belief as such, it was of experience, the real experience of little arrows from the spirit realm.

It was not just spirit arrows which linked these ancient experiences of disease. Certain illnesses were themselves believed to be 'alive,' not just as energy but as real identities from the Otherworld which required negotiation and communication to reveal why they had chosen to attack the poor victim, and how they could be encouraged to leave. There is a theme here of invasion by an exterior energy or entity, which is very much alive, and which aims to take possession of the body. Perhaps the entity has a message to convey, or perhaps it is simply that the host caused an insult to the elves, either way, illness was a living thing.

Hundreds of years later this theme remains valid. Modern medicine now knows that many illnesses are indeed caused by an invasion of bacteria or viruses which are very much alive, and these unwelcome invaders appear focused on their intent to take over our bodies and diminish our health. Sometimes we are told that perhaps we caught our cold because we were 'run down' and have not been taking care of ourselves as we should. We sometimes say therefore, that the cold was trying to tell us something important about our lifestyle. Many other illnesses seem to be equally informative with their own personal message to deliver. We are eating too much sugar, we are drinking too much alcohol, we require greater rest, *ad finitum*......We may not conceptualise or experience our bacterial invasions as the work of disgruntled elves, but perhaps if we did then a greater choice of healing remedies would be revealed.

Today we are encouraged by 'new-age' practitioners to engage with our illnesses, to go inside and talk with them, and imagine the disease becoming weaker and weaker whilst utilising positive thinking exercises to increase our psychic defences against the nasty illness. All such teachings are valuable yet they miss one essential point, they assume that the illness is *ours*, that it *belongs* to us, and we must use the power of thought to diminish it.

The problem is, when we identify with the illness in this way, we lose the fight. We have taken it as our own forgetting it to be an identity in its own right. This is not to say that no sympathetic relationship exists between the illness and ourselves, as already stated, the illness is there for a reason however, we must not *own it* entirely. Bring back the elves!

In the Lacnunga there is healing spell to cure the patient of an attack from '*the race of elves*'. It was recorded that the wicce would take various herbs including the hop, lupine, vervain, viper's bugloss, leek, garlic and cleavers and put '*the herbs in a vessel.*' The wicce would then chant above the herbs whilst mixing them with melting butter/fat and straining the mixture through fine muslin. The patient would be directed to apply the subsequent balsam to the area which was painful and this it was believed, would soothe the wounds from the 'elf-shot' (*ylfa gescot* in Old English).

The wicce may send the patient away with a charm to protect them from potential vengeance from the slighted elves. A charm does not cure the current affliction, but is designed to protect from future ones. A specific charm against elves of ill intent uses Mugwort:

'Remember, Mugwort, what you revealed,
What you set out in mighty revelation.
Una you are called, oldest of plants,
You have might against three and against thirty,
You have might against poison and against infection,
You have might against the evil that travels around the land'

(And as it appears in Old English in the Lacnunga manuscript):

'Gemyne ðu mucgwyrt hwæt þu ameldodest,
Hwæt þu renadest æt regenmelde.
Una þu hattest yldost wyrta,
þu miht wið iii wið xxx,
þu miht wiþ attre ond wið onflyge
þu miht wiþ þa laþan ðe geond lond fereð.'

An invocation such as this would 'compel the herb' to reveal and activate its inner nature of protection. We see here how the wicce did not impose their will upon the herb and 'charge' it with power as we tend to do today, in our implicit Christianised belief of human God given dominion over the natural world. Rather, they met the herb within the space of imagination, and compelled it with invocation to reveal its power which was already alive and potent within it. Note that the invocation appeals to what the herb itself has made known, what it has revealed about its nature and once revealed, the power could then be magically directed.

The innate power of herbs was often harnessed and utilised within protective charms and amulets, and a very famous example has been immortalised within the classic children's nursery rhyme '*ring a ring o' roses*' where playground children dance in a circle whilst singing:

"Ring a ring o' roses, a pocket full of posies, a-tishoo! a-tishoo! we all fall down!"

Although conflicting origins for this rhyme abound, it is commonly thought to have been a representation of the symptoms of the Black Death, the plague which exterminated millions of people during the fourteenth century. The 'ring of roses' may have referred to the first signs of the round red *buboes,* which are the swollen lymph glands giving the plague its title of bubonic, and the sneezing refers to the final stages of bronchial distress before the almost inevitable conclusion of death. Of interest for this discussion however, is the *pocket full of posies.*

Although historians attribute the carrying of herbs to a desire for an ancient type of deodorant, this conclusion seems unsound as archaeological and anthropological research suggests that our ancestors of the time tended to burn aromatic herbs predominantly within the home to counter the all too familiar smells of the period, raw sewage, rotting waste etc. Personal deodorising was not yet a priority. However, carrying sweet smelling herbs upon the person was known to have been a common type of healing amulet.

The plague was a disease specifically associated with bad odours, as the body of the cruelly afflicted would putrefy from the inside out causing the most abominable stench which it is told, could be smelt for miles. Knowing what we now do regarding the status and identity of disease to our ancestors, we can consider with some confidence that the entity which they believed to be responsible for the plague was a particularly evil daemon, which was in its element and very happy with foul stenches. The logical response of the people therefore, was to make themselves less attractive to its advances by carrying a magical sweet smelling charm, encouraging it to seek its invasion elsewhere.

The innate power of herbs fascinated the great first century Roman historian Pliny. Pliny was a man obsessed with collecting knowledge which included detailed first hand observations of the indigenous cultures of Northern Europe. He would send his scholars with the Roman armies to record every detail about the peoples they encountered and specifically, their religious and magical practices. Within Pliny's observations in England he says of the herb vervain, '*When it was rubbed on the body all wishes were granted; it dispelled fevers and other maladies; it was an antidote against snakes, and conciliated hearts*'. Vervain also protected against fear and fantasy, as did holding five leaves from the nettle in the hand.

Pliny further describes that the herb selago was believed by the Angles to have '*preserved one from accident, and its smoke when burned healed maladies of the eye*' and also '*The diggers do not face the wind, they first trace round the plant three circles with a sword, and then dig up the plant whilst facing west ... They then pound root, with rose oil and wine, it cures fluxes and pain in the eyes.*' He further commented that the indigenous wicce collected these herbs specifically without the use of an iron tool, and

19

accompanied the collection with an offering of bread. It is quite possible this indicates how many of these practices, or certainly elements of them, pre-date the discovery of iron, and the offering of bread suggests that a real entity requires respect.

The wicce's use of healing herbs was also observed by the later Christians who widely documented their usage from the ancient Britons, Celts and Anglo-Saxons, before the Roman Church developed its overt taste for repression and sources became either Christianised or eliminated. The Saint Hildegard of Bingen, writing in the early twelfth century, was fascinated by the application of herbs, and within her *Physica* she records the ancient practices and beliefs concerning healing magic:

'If a depression conditioned by various fever attacks cause a person headaches, he should take mallow and twice the amount of sage, crush these into a pulp in a mortar and pour some olive oil upon it. If there is no oil, a little vinegar will do. He should then apply it over the skull from the forehead to the neck and wrap a cloth over it. He should do this for three days. During these three days he should add fresh olive oil or fresh vinegar in the evening and continue this until he gets better. For mallow juice releases the bile; however, the sap of the sage dries it up, the olive oil anoints the afflicted head, and the vinegar draws out the bitterness from the bile.'

Hildegard amassed a wealth of healing materials from the indigenous pre-Christian peoples of England and Northern Europe, and she appears to have been particularly interested in mandrake, explaining the applications of the herb at some length. The mandrake *'is hot at first .....and is formed from the earth from which Adam was made. It looks like a person but is a herb that comes in two forms: one is the man, the other the woman; the form of the woman is somewhat nicer.'* Hildegard goes on to list the various healing attributes of mandrake as follows:

'It should be known that mandrake is good to use for all trembling.

Whoever has a headache, from whichever disorder it comes, he should eat from the head-like part of the herb, however much he wants, [and] it will be reduced......he who has a pain in the throat should eat from the throat and the pain will go from him....whatever kind of pain the person has, he should eat of the herb from the place where the similarity lies, it aids his health..... Mandrake is good against poison...It is good against disorders of the liver....it is also good against disorders of the loins....disorders of the lungs...It also reduces swelling of the spleen.'

Hildegard goes on to describe how the spirit dwelling in mandrake is essentially an evil spirit, '*the devil lies therein and his spirit is there ......[it] has a great deal of evil with it, as sometimes happens with idols*'. She advises therefore that one should '*dig this herb out, and one should throw it into a spring for a day and a night; thus the water takes all evil humours out, so it is therefore no longer good for evil doing.*' With the water having purified the mandrake and expelled the devil, the herb can no longer be used for ill against another.

Her account of an inherent evil within mandrake, which Hildegard connects similarly to the evil within idols, may indicate the neo-Platonist belief which survived within some factions of the early church, that representations are illusions which Christians then believed were deceptions sent from the Devil. Mandrake may have been seen as the devil's attempt to appear in human form and therefore, present a perversion of Christ who was believed to be God incarnated in human form.

Hildegard's account goes into even more detail regarding the process of working healing spells with mandrake, and here follows two spells that she documented in some detail.

1. A healing spell for persons suffering from 'uncouthness' of spirit

For a man who *"cannot control himself and is uncouth from*

sinful ways or from the uncouthness of burning heat [lust], *he should take the female form of mandrake, to cleanse it in water, as I have described earlier, and cut from it that [part] which is between the breast and navel... and bind it on his navel for three days and three nights.. Then to cut the same piece in half and bind a piece on each hip for three days and three nights. Powder also the left hand of the herb, add a small amount of camphor to the powder.. and eat it... so his impure desires will be reduced."*

For *"a woman who cannot control her uncouthness she should take the herb mandrake, which has the man's form, and work with it in a similar manner to that written before: but the powder should be from the right hand."*

2. A healing spell for depression and worry

'Whoever has a depressed nature or sadness and worry in the heart, he should lay the mandrake, which has been cleansed, next to him in his bed. So that the mandrake heats up with his sweating, and speaks thus; "God, who from the earth made men on earth without pain, I lay now next to me this earth, which has never corrupted, that my earth also feels joy as you intended." You will then feel the depression leave you and joy fill your heart.' Hildegard indicates that if you do not have mandrake then the *'fruits of the tree called Fagus [or the] Cedar tree or Aspen'* will work as a substitute.

Although her writing dates from the twelfth century it is certain that these observations embody a far older pre-Christian tradition of healing Craft. Hildegard is remarkably unbiased in her writing, including far fewer examples of Christianisation of source materials than many of her colleagues and contemporaries. The spells and magic workings she describes contain every aspect of the ancient healing practices of the wicce.

Adjurations for example, were an important component of ancient healing practices and remain central to the healing Craft today. The words spoken or chanted serve as a command to the spirit or entity which is believed to be attacking the person, to leave the host immediately. The following example of a healing adjuration within the Lacnunga demands the spirit to behave in certain ways which will bring about its own demise and therefore, restore healing and health. The adjuration is for the healing of a cyst or tumour:

'*May you be consumed as coal upon the hearth. May you shrink as dung upon a wall. And may you dry up as water in a pail. May you become as small as a linseed grain, and much smaller than the hipbone of an itch-mite, and may you become so small that you become nothing.*'

This command for the cyst to behave as does the water in a pail or dung upon a wall, demonstrates a further element of magical healing and magical processes generally. The cyst's presence is being imaginatively likened to water for example, which if left in a pail will disappear through evaporation. A sympathetic connection is being conjured between the spirit of the cyst and the physical element of water, and then this allegorical relationship, once established by engaging the imaginative faculty, can be utilised to bring a corresponding behaviour from the Otherworldly spirit. A sympathetic identity between the two elements is imaginatively constructed to direct the spirit of the cyst to act and behave in a certain way.

In Hildegard's spells we clearly see how the parts of the mandrake are sympathetically related to the parts of the person which require healing. The energetic link is more certain here as the herb does indeed resemble quite strikingly, the human form. Similarity and relationship, whether overt or allegorical is of utmost importance, and can be utilised in many magical ways as further chapters will explore. However, this sympathetic identity magic can also be used to bring about the opposite of healing, as this report from fourteenth century Coventry in England

23

describes.

The report centres upon a familiar case of two neighbours who were involved in a dispute. However, unlike today where we may approach a legal solution or mediation, one of the neighbours sought the advice of their local wicce who suggested a rather different course of action. The neighbour was instructed to make a waxen image of the other person, as like to the other as possible and then to drive a lead spike into the head. The effect was immediate and had the consequence of sending the neighbour completely mad.

After some days, the waxen image was used again although this time a second lead nail was driven through the heart. Again the magic was immediate and the neighbour fell down dead. The dispute was resolved. No further details remain although we may deduce that other magical processes were perhaps used to strengthen the sympathetic link between the wax image and the neighbour. We can see how representations can be used effectively, not just for healing but for any other purpose which requires a link of identity. Hildegard's concern with the innate evil of mandrake was perhaps strengthened due to these darker types of practice employed by disputing neighbours or those in similar circumstances!

A further type of magical process occurs within the second of Hildegard's healing spells. The mandrake is connected to the patient by laying it next to him, and allowing it to heat up to his body temperature and thus to bathe in his own sweat. The adjuration compels the essential nature of mankind which is without pain to be restored, and resemble once more the uncorrupted state of the earthy mandrake. The mandrake is thus used as a catalyst to absorb the illness from the 'earthiness' of the patient and this transference of spirit energy is another common feature in wicce healing spells.

The transference of spirit energy was documented within

the practices of an Italian witch of the fifteenth century called Matteuccia Francisci. Matteuccia was famous for teaching healing spells, and one of her instructions which still survives, was considered by her to be a good general cure for all types of illness. The patient was to take '*a bone from an unbaptised baby out to a crossroad, burying it there, and saying various prayers and formulas on that spot over nine days.*'

Mainly however, she would prescribe the transfer of illness from the patient to an object, even if that object was another person. She is reported to have cured a patient's lameness by brewing together thirty different types of herb into a potion whilst chanting incantations over the cauldron of steaming liquid. She then took the potion and poured it out onto the street so that whoever should next pass by would receive the spirit of lameness. Thus the spirit would find another home having been compelled and adjured to transfer to an alternative and unsuspecting host.

The practice of magical transference has led many modern spiritual teachers to argue our ancestors to have possessed a rather simple and ignorant cosmology, which fails to perceive the reality of the infinite universe. Our new-age teachers ascribe to what appears to be the eastern view that energy is abundant and infinite within our universe, and the more you work with energy the more energy you create. This certainly appears contrary to the wicce who transferred energy thus giving the appearance of a people who viewed energy as a finite and limited resource. This view of our ancestors is however, uninformed and misguided.

The wicce saw the Otherworld as a constant flowing of infinite energy and power which could be directed and utilised. However, they differentiated this essential flowing energy from the spirits who inhabited the Otherworld, and at times chose to come into our world and inhabit physical matter such as the human body. The wicce observed how such an invasion diminished or blocked the life force of the person within whom the spirit had decided to dwell. In order for the life force, the abundant energy of the creative universe to flow once more within the body of the person, the troublesome spirit must be exorcised or transferred elsewhere. An abundant energetic universe is not therefore, as many are inclined to believe, an Eastern import. There are many ways in which the wicce worked with the infinite flowing energy from the Otherworld, often presenting a far more sophisticated understanding than that of the Eastern traditions.

The wicce were intimately attuned to the energy emanating from the Otherworld and its effects within our physical reality. They sensed when this flowing had become blocked, and they also recognised the times when the veils between the two worlds were more permeable, or more suited to certain types of magical practices. For example, there were many ritual observances afforded to the collection of herbs and their use.

The moon and its phases were often utilised for their powerful effects. Specifically, in healing spells the moon was associated with the mind and unconscious, so appeals to lunar energy were thought to create a sympathetic healing bond with those afflicted by mental illness. For example, a person suffering from such an illness of mind may be prescribed a bundle of herbs allied to the moon, which were to be collected at the new moon just before dawn, wrapped in red cloth and tied about the patient's head whilst the moon was waxing. The waxing moon has long been known as a time for increasing the potency of magical workings and as a particularly good time for healing spells. To banish a spirit or daemon thought to be causing a mental illness however, the spell would be worked in the waning moon to aid the diminishing of the mischievous sprite's power.

A further healing spell which utilises the moon's phases is recorded in the Lacnunga and concerns the collection of the herbs periwinkle and mulberry. Periwinkle should be plucked *'when the moon is nine nights old, and eleven nights, and thirteen nights, and thirty nights, and when it is one night old.'* Mulberry should be collected *'when to all men the moon is seventeen nights old, after the meeting of the sun, ere the rising of the moon.'*

Herbs would generally be collected at dawn or just before the sunrise. The moments between the night and the day were known to be especially powerful and potent times of Otherworldly connection. The night was symbolic of that which is hidden from our physical eyes, and thus the moment of dawn represents the transition of knowledge from the occult to the revealed. Herbs harvested at such a time would retain the power of their Otherwordly spirit which would be revealed and compelled by the wicce for magical healing purposes in the material world. Transition times within the turning of the year were also viewed as very powerful. Winter was a time of sleep and gestation, when life was hidden beneath the ground, awaiting the light of summer's sun to bring it into manifestation.

In the Lacnunga there is a spell for a cyst or tumour upon the neck which utilises the turning from spring into summer. The herbs which include neck-wort, boar- throat, brown-wort and farthing-wort, are to be collected in equal quantities on the three nights leading up to the summer solstice. The herbs should be made into a concoction to be drunk at dawn. One sip at the first cock crow, a second sip at dawn and then at sunrise proper he should finish the drink entirely and rest thereafter. Here we can see that the hidden natures of the herbs are to be digested directly into the body of the afflicted person at the moment of daylight's revealing.

The Lacnunga also recommends that when prescribing sea-holly for healing, *'thou shalt take up this wort with its roots, then beware that no sun shine upon it, lest its beauty and its might be spoiled through the brightness of the sun,'* implying that many herbs were considered to be at their most efficacious whilst still cloaked within the veil of the Otherworld.

A direction for the use of bark within remedies was rather different however, with ash and oak to be collected from the side of the tree which faced east towards the rising sun. It is often thought by scholars that this is because the east side of the tree receives the greatest amount of sunlight and is therefore strengthened in life force. I consider it equally likely however, that the east side of the tree is where the tree spirit is first witness to the change from dark to light and the knowledge that this transient moment reveals.

What follows is a selection of healing remedies, charms and spells direct from Bald's Leechbook Book III and a few from the Lacnunga too. There are hundreds of cures and charms but I hope I have selected the best here. I cannot say that I have tried all of these and thankfully, have had no cause to. I reproduce these as informative and cannot and would not recommend that you use them (indeed some ingredients are known to be poisonous), always of course, seek out a modern medical professional if you are suffering from an illness of any kind. The translations are presented by kind permission of Stephen Pollington.

I present the charms in three sections with the first group focusing upon issues surrounding childbirth and menstruation. Midwifery remained under the auspices of women far into the conversion times when the imposition of classical medical learning began to empower the emerging and exclusively male physicians. Childbirth and menstruation were still areas of mystery and fear, an area to which the wicce were still called by those men too afraid of what goes on in the depths of femininity. The second group of charms deals with the mischievous acts of elves and devils and we can begin to see the very real presence such creatures had for our ancestors. The final section contains remedies for more general medical complaints such as haemorrhoids and rashes.

Some of the charms are purely medical whilst others contain references to magical and ritualistic practices. Healing was a fundamental concern for our ancestors just as it is for us today, and we are very fortunate that these medico-magical healing spells were recorded. They are arguably the only real and tangible insight we have into our indigenous magical past, where healing was still regarded as a magical transformative act. Within some of these charms we find obvious examples of Christianisation and can only speculate therefore, regarding the original heathen directions.

For general difficulties during childbirth and pregnancy

Wiþ þon þe wif ne mæge bearn acennan nim feldmoran nioþowearde, wyl on meolcum ond on wætre, do begea emfela, sele etan þa moran ond þæt wos supan. To þon olcan bind on þæt winstre þeoh up wið þæt cennende lim nioþowearde beolonan oþþe xii corn cellendran sædes ond þæt sceal don cniht oððe mæden. Swa þæt bearn sie acenned do þa wyrta aweg þy læs þæt innelfe utsige. Gif of wife nelle gan æfter þam beorþre þæt gecyndelic sie, seoþe eald spic on wætre, beþe mid þone cwiþ oððe hleomoc oþþe hocces leaf wyl on ealoþ, sele drincan hit hat. Gif on wife sie dead bearn wyl on meolce ond on wætre hleomoc ond polleian, sele drincan on dæg tuwa. Georne is to wyrnanne bearneacnum wife þæt hio aht sealtes ete oððe swetes, oþþe beor drince, ne swines flæac ete, ne naht fætes, ne of hire sie ær riht tide. Gif hio blede to swiþe æfter þam beorþre nioþowearde clatan wyl on meolce, sele etan ond supan þæt wos.

For that a woman be unable to bear a child, take the lower part of parsnip, boil it in milk and in water, add equal amounts of both, give the roots to eat and the juice to sip. For the same, bind on the left thigh, up against the genital area, the lower part of henbane or twelve grains of coriander seed, and a boy or girl must do it; as the child is born, take the plants away lest the innards come out. If what is natural will not go out of the woman after the childbirth, boil old bacon in water, bathe the vagina with it, or with speedwell or leaf of hock, boil it in ale, give it to drink hot. If a dead child be in a woman, boil in milk and in water speedwell, and pennyroyal, give it to drink twice a day. Earnestly one must refuse a pregnant woman that she should eat anything salty, nor anything sweet, nor drink beer, nor eat pig's flesh, nor anything fatty, nor drink till she be drunk, nor travel afar, nor ride too vigorously on a horse, lest the baby come away from her before the right time. If she should bleed too much after the childbirth, boil the lower part of burdock in milk, give it to eat and the juice to drink.

A remedy for morning sickness

Wið morgenwlætunga, wyl on wætre eorþgeallen, swet mid hunige, sele him godne bollan fulne on morgenne.

Against morning sickness: boil earthnavel in water, sweeten with honey; give [her?] a good bowl full in the morning.

For a barren woman or one who cannot nourish a child

Gif wif ne mæge bearn beran, se wifmann we hire cild afedan ne mæg, gange to gewitenes mannes birgenne ond stæppe þonne þriwa ofer þa byrgenne ond cweðe þonne þriwa þas word: "þis me to bote þære laþan lætbyrde, þis me to bote þære swæran swærtbyrde, þis me to bote þære laðan lambyrde" ond þonne þæt wif seo mid berane ond heo to hyre hlaforde on reste ga, þonne cweþe heo: "up ic gonge, ofer þe stæppe mid cwican cilde, nalæs mid cwellendum, mid fulborenum, nalæs mis fægan" ond þonne seo modor gefele þæt bearn si cwic, ga þonne to cyrican ond þonne heo toforan þan weofode cume cweþe þonne: "criste ic sæde þis acyþed."

If a woman cannot bear a child: Let the woman who cannot nourish her child go to the grave of a dead man and then step three times over the grave and say these words three times: "This is a relief to me for the hateful slow birth, this is a relief to me for the sad stillbirth, this is a relief to me for the hateful lame birth." And when the woman will be with child and goes to bed, to her husband, then she is to say: "Up I go, step over you, with a living child not a dying [one], with a full-born [one] not with a doomed [one]" and when the mother feels that the child is alive, she is to go then to a church and when she comes before the altar she is to then say: "To Christ I said, declared this."

A remedy for painful breasts

Wið breostwærce, marubie, nefte, ontre, bisceopwyrt, wenwyrt, wyl on hunige ond buteran, do þæs huniges twæde ond þære buteran þriddan dæl, nytta swa þe þearf sie.

For breast pain, horehound, catmint, radish, bishopwort, wenwort, boil in honey and butter, put two thirds of honey to one third of butter, use it as it may be needful to you.

To relieve womb and stomach pains

Wiþ wambewærce ond ryselwærce þær þu geseo tordwifel on eorþan up weorpan ymbfo hine mid twam handum mid his geweorpe, wafa mid þinum handum swiþe ond cweð þriwa: Remedium facio ad uentris dolorem. Weorp þonne oferbæc þone wifel on wge, beheald þæt þu ne locige æfter. Ðonne monnes wambewærce oððe rysle, ymbfoh mid þinum handum þa wambe, him bið sona sel, xii. Monaþ þu meaht swa don æfter þam wifele.

For womb pain and stomach pain, where you see a dungbeetle on the ground casting it up, surround it with your two hands, with it upcast, wave vigorously with your hands and say thrice: "Remedium facio ad uentris dolorem" then throw the weevil away backwards, make sure that you do not look at it; then surround the person's womb or stomach pain with your hands, the womb will soon do better. You may do this for twelve months after the weevil.

A further remedy for womb pain

Wiþ wambewærce ofgeot polleian ond drince ond sume binde to þam nafolan ond wite georne þæt sio wyrt aweg ne aglide; sona bið sel.

For womb pain, steep pennyroyal and let him [her] drink it, and bind some to his [her] navel, and be certain that the plant should not slip away; it will soon be better.

(Author's note- DO NOT be tempted to try this remedy for period pain dear sisters! Pennyroyal was also taken to induce miscarriage and abortion.)

To induce menstruation

Wiþ þon þe wifum sie forstanden hira monaþ gecynd wyl on ealað hleomac ond twa curmeallan, sele drincan ond beþe þæt wif on hatum baþe ond drince þone drenc on þam baþe. Hafa þe ær geworht clam of beordræstan ond of grenre mucgwyrte ond merce ond of berene melwe, meng ealle tosomme, gehrer on pannan, clæm on þæt gecynde lim ond þone cwið nioþoweardne þonne hio of þam baðe gæþ ond drince scenc fulne þæs ilcan drenches wearmes ond bewreoh þæt wif wel ond læt beon swa beclæmed lange tide þæs dæges, do swa tuwa swa þriwa swæþer þu scyle; þu scealt simle þam wife bæþ wyrcean ond drenc sellan on þa ilcan tid þe hire sio gecynd æt wære, ahsa þæs æt þam wife. Gif wife to swiþe offlowe sio monað gecynd genim niwe horses tord, lege on hate gleda, læt reocan swiþe betweoh þa þeoh up under þæt hrægl þæt se mon swæte swiþe.

For that their menstrual be absent from women, boil in ale speedwell and the two centauries, give it to drink and bathe the woman in a hot bath, and let her drink the drink in the bath; have already made for yourself a poultice from beer dregs and from green mugwort and wild celery, and from barley meal, mix them all together, stir together in a pan, daub it onto the genital area and onto the lower part of the vagina, when she gets out of the bath, and let her drink a cupful of the same drink warm, and cover the woman well and let her be thus daubed for a long time in the day, do thus twice or thrice as you may have to; you must always make the bath and give the drink to the woman at the same time as would be normal for her [menstruation], ask this [time] of the woman. If the menstruals flow too strongly from a woman, take fresh horse droppings, lay it onto hot coals, let it smoke well between the thighs upwards under the clothing so that the person should sweat greatly.

A remedy for a woman unable to produce breast milk for her baby

Se wifman se ne mæge bearn afedan nime þonne anes bleoos cu meoluc on hyre handa ond gesupe þonne mid hyre muþe ond gange þonne to to yrnendum wætere ond spiwa þærin þa meolc ond hlade þonne mid þære ylcan hand þoþs wæteres muðfulne ond forwelge, cweþe þonne þas word: "gehwer freed ic me þone mæran magapihtan mis þysse mæran metepihtan þone ic me wille habban ond ham gan.", þonne heo to þan broce ga, þonne ne beseo heo no, ne eft þonne heo þanan ga, ond þonne ga heo in oþer hus oþer he out ofeode ond þær gebyrge metes.

The woman who cannot nourish her child: let her then take milk from a cow of one colour in her hand and sip it up with her mouth and go then to running water and spit the milk into it and take up with the same hand a mouthful of the water and swallow it; let her then say these words: "Everywhere I have carried the splendid stomach-strong with this splendid well-fed [one] which I wish to have for myself and go home." When she will go to the brook, she must not look about at all, nor when she will go back; and let her then go into another house than the one she left and take food there.

With regard to this final female charm it is suggested by Tony

Linsell that a cow of just one colour was probably quite rare in dark ages England and thus the milk from such a cow was probably considered to be purer than the milk of a dual coloured cow. To draw the evil spirit out of her own milk the woman would have sipped the cow's milk in order to transfer the spirit into that before spitting the spirit into the running water to be cleansed. Not looking about her would be to ensure the spirit being carried in the water could not jump back into her again and infect her milk once more. To go home to a different house would confuse the spirit if it did indeed try to find her again.

A cure for madness and possession from devils

Wiþ deofle, liþedrenc ond ungemynde: do on ealu cassuc, elehtran moran, finul, ontre, betonice, hindheolope, merce, rude, wermod, nefte, elene, ælfþone, wulfes comb; gesing xii mæssan ofer þam drence ond drince, him biþ sona sel. Drenc wiþ deofles costunga: þefan þorn, cropleac, eletre, ontre, bisceopwyrt, finul, cassuc, betonice, gehalga þas wyrta, do on ealu halig wæter, ond sie se drenc þærinne þær se seoca man sie, ond simle ær þon þe he drince, sing þriwa ofer þam drence: dues in nomine tuo saluum me fac.

For a devil and for madness, a mild drink: put into ale hassock, lupin's roots, fennel, radish, betony, hindhealth, marche, rue, wormwood, catmint, elecampane, elfthon, wolf's comb; sing twelve masses over the drink and let him drink it; it will soon be better for him. A drink for the devil's temptations: hawthorn, cropleek, lupin, radish, bishopwort, fennel, hassock, betony; hallow these plants, put holy water into ale and let the drink be inside where the sick person is, and always before he may drink it, sing thrice over the drink "dues in nomine tuo me fac."

For elf-sickness

Wið ælfadle nim bisceopwyrt, finul elehtre, ælfþonan niopowearde, ond gehalgodes cristes, mæles ragu, ond stor, do ælcre hand fulle, bebind ealle þa wyrta on claþe, bedyp on fontwætre gehalgodum þriwa, læt singan ofer iii mæssan, ane omnibus Scis oþre contra tribulatjonem, þriddan pro inwirmis; do þonne gleda an gledfæt ond lege þa wyrta on, gerec þone man mid þam wyrtum ær undern ond on niht ond sing letania ond credan ond pater noster ond writ him cristes mæl on ælcum lime ond nim lytle hand fulle þæs ilcan cynnes wyrta gelice gehalgode ond wyl on meolce, dryp þriwa gehalgodes wætres on ond supe ær his mete, him biþ sona sel.

For elf-sickness, take bishopwort, fennel, lupin, the lower part of elfthon, lichen from the hallowed sign of Christ, and storax, take a handful of each, bind up all the plants in a cloth, dip it into hallowed font water thrice, have three masses sung over it: first 'omnibus sanctus', second 'contra tribulationem', third 'pro inwirmis', then put hot coals into a censer, and lay the plants on it; smoke the man with the plants before morning and at night, and sing the litany and the credo and 'pater noster' and mark Christ's sign on each limb, and take a small handful of plants of the same kind, likewise hallowed, and boil them in milk, drip hallowed water in thrice, and let him sip it before his food, it will soon be better for him.

A further charm for elf-sickness

Eft wiþ þon lege under weofod þas wyrte, læt gesingan ofer viiii mæssan: recels, halig sealt, iii heafod cropleaces, ælfþonan nioþewearde, elenan, nim on morgen scenc fulne meoluce, dryp þriwa haliges wæteres on, supe swa he hatost mæge, ete mid iii snæde ælfþonan ond þonne he restan wille hæbbe gleda þærinne, lege stor ond ælfþonan on þa gleda ond re chine mid þæt he swæte, ond þæt hus geond rec ond georne þone man gesena ond þonne he on reste gange ete iii snæda eolonan, ond iii cropleaces, ond iii sealtes, ond hæbbe him scenc fulne ealað ond drype þriwa haliy wæter on, besupe ælce snæd, gereste hine siþþan, do þis viiii morgenas, ond viiii niht, him biþ sona sel.

Again for that [elf-sickness], lay these plants under the altar, have nine masses sung over them: incense, holy salt, three heads of cropleek, the lower part of elfthon, elecampane, take a cupful of milk in the morning, drip holy water in thrice, let him sip it as hot as he can, let him eat with it three slices of elfthon and when he wishes to rest let him have coals therein, lay storax and elfthon onto the coals, and steam him with it so that he may sweat and let it steam throughout the house, and sign the man earnestly, and when he goes to his rest let him eat three morsels of elecampane, and three of cropleek and three of salt and let him have a cupful of ale and drip holy water into it thrice, let him swallow each morsel and let him rest himself afterwards, do this for nine mornings and nine nights, it will soon be better for him.

For one bound by witchcraft

Gyf hwa on þære untrumnysse sy þæt he sy cis, þonne meaht ðu hine unbindan; genim þysse wyrte þe we leonfot nemdon fif ðyfelas butan wyrttruman, seoð on wætere on wanwægendum monan ond ðweah hine þærmid ond læd ut of þam huse on foran nihte ond ster hyne þære wyrte þe man aristolochiam nemneð ond þonne he utga ne beseo he hyne nu on bæc; þus ðu hine meaht of þære untrumnysse unbindan.

If someone be in the affliction that he be 'bewitched' you can unbind him then; take five bushes of this plant which we named lionfoot, boil in water under a waning moon and wash him with it and lead him out of the house before nightfall and waft him with the plant which is called *aristolochiam* (smearwort) and when he goes out let him not look back, thus you can unbind him from the affliction.

A cure for 'water-elf sickness' (author's note- a sickness brought on by drinking foul and dirty water or a wound which has become infected by foul water)

Gif mon biþ on wæterælfadle þonne him þa handnæglas wonne ond þa Eagan tearige ond wile locian niþer, do him þis to lædedome: eoforþrote, caauc, fone niopoweard, eowberge, elehtre, eolone, merscmealwan crop, fenminte, dile, lilie, attorlaþe, polleie, murubie, docce, Ellen, felterre, wermod, streawbergean leaf, consoled, ofgeot mid ealaþ, do halig wæter to, sing þis gealdor ofer þriwa: Je binne awrat, betestbeadowræda, swa benne ne burnon, ne burston, ne fundian ne feologan, ne hoppetan, ne wund Waco sian, ne dolh diopian, ac him self healed hale wæge, ne ace þe þon ma þe eorpan on eare ace. Sing þis manegum siþum: eorþe þe on bere ealle hire mihtum ond magenum; þas galdor mon mæg singan on.

If someone should be in water-elf sickness then his fingernails will be pale, and eyes watery and he will look downwards. Do this for him as a leechdom: boarthroat, hassock, the lower part of iris, yewberry, lupin, elecampane, a sprig of dwarf elder, felter, wormwood, strawberry leaf, comfrey; pour out with ale, add holy [blessed] water, sing this charm over it thrice: "I wreathed the wound, best of battlegroups, so injuries should not burn, nor burst, nor spread, nor fade, nor throb, nor the wound be weak, nor the scar deepen, but keep for itself the blessed vessel, nor ache any more than earth would ache in the ear." Sing this many times: "May Earth bear you up with all her powers and might." These charms one may sing onto the wound.

(Author's note- leechcraft/leechdom was a term used to describe the ancient herb craft specific to England and has nothing to do with leeches!)

To protect against nightwalkers

Wyrc sealfle wið nihtgengan, wyl on buteran elehtran, hegerifan, bisceopwyrt, reade magþan, cropleac, sealt, smire mid, him bið sona sel.

Make a salve for nightgoers: boil in butter lupin, hedge rive, bishopwort, red maythe, cropleek, salt; smear with it, it will soon be better for him.

(Author's note- I will return to 'nightwalkers' in chapter four!)

For a woman's madness

Wiþ wifgemædlan geberge on neaht nestig rædices moran, þy dæge ne mæg þe se gemædla sceþþan.

For a woman's madness, let her eat radish's root at night having fasted, for that day the madness may not harm you.

A general tonic to ward off all illness

Wið adle, nim þreo leaf gageles on gewylledre mealtre meolce, syle þry morhgenas drincan.

Against illness: take three leaves of gale in boiled sour milk; give it to him to drink for three mornings.

To cure a rash

Wið oman, genim ane grene gyred ond læt sittan þone man on middan huses flore, ond bestric hine ymbutan ond cweð o pars et o uilia pars et pars inopia est, alfa et o, initium et finis.

Against a rash: take one green rod and have the man sit in the middle of the house's floor, and strike a circle around him and say: "Oh part, and O vile part, and the part is useless; alpha and omega, beginning and end."

A cure for haemorrhoids

Gif se uic weorðe on mannes setle geseten, þonne nim ðu clatan moran, þa greatan, iii oððe iiii, ond berec hy on hate æmergean, ond ateoh þonne ða ane of ðan heorðe ond cnuca ond wyrc swylce an lytel cicel, ond lege to þæm setle swa ðu hatost forberan mæge, þonne se cicel colige, þonne wyrc þu ma ond lege to, ond beo on stilnesse dæg oððe twegen, þonne þu þis do, hit is afandad lǽcecraft, ne delfe hy nan man þa moran mid isene, ond mod wǽtere ne þwea, ac strice hy mid claðe clǽne, ond do swiþe þynne cla∂ betweonan þǽt setl ond ∂one cicel.

If the haemorrhoid grow on a man's seat: then take burdock's roots, three or four of the large ones, and smoke them over hot embers; then take one out from the hearth, and pound it and make it like a little cake; and lay it onto the seat, as hot as you can bear it; when the cake cools, then make more and lay them on, and be in peace for a day or two; when you do this, it is tested leechcraft, let no man dig up the roots with iron, nor wash them in water, but wipe them clean with a cloth; and put a thin cloth between the seat and the cake.

To cure a bleeding mouth

Wi∂ þon þe mon blode wealle þurh his mu∂, genim betonican þreora trymessa gewǽge ond cole gate meoloc þreo cuppan fulle, ond drice, þonne bi∂ he sona hal.

Against when blood pours through his mouth: take three tremisses' weight of betony and three cups full of cool goat's milk, and let him drink; then he will soon be healthy.

For an adder's bite

Wi∂ nǽddran slite genim þas ylcan wyrte þe we ebulum nemdun ond ǽr þam ∂e þu hy forceorfe heald hy on þinre handa ond cwe∂ þriwa nigon siþan, omnes malas bestias canto þǽt ys þonne on ure geþeode, besing ond ofercum ealle yfele wilddeor, forceorf hy ∂onne mis swyþe cearpon sexe on þry dǽlas. Ond þa hwile þe þu ∂is do þenc be þam men þe þu ∂ǽrmid þencst to gelacnienne ond þonne þu þanon wende ne beseoh þu þe na; nim ∂onne þa wyrte ond cnuca hy, lege to þam slite, sona he bi∂ hal.

For an adder's bite take this same plant which is called 'ebulum' and before you cut it hold it in your hand and say thrice times: "Omnes malas bestias canto" which is in our language "I charm and overcome all evil wild beasts" then cut it up with a very sharp knife into three parts, and while you are doing this think of the person whom you intend to cure therewith, and when you turn from there do not look back at all; then take the plant and pound it, lay it to the bite, he will shortly be well.

A remedy for asthma

Wið angcbreoste, wyll holenrinde on gate meolce ond sup wearm nyhstig.

Against asthma: boil holly-bark in goat's milk and sip it warm, having fasted.

A cure for fainting attacks

Wið ðone swiman, nim rudan ond salfian ond finul ond eorðfig, bettonican ond lilian, cnuca ealle pas wyrta tosomne, do on ænne pohchan, ofgeot mid wætere, grid swyðe, læt sigan ut on sum fæt, nim þone wætan ond wyrm, ond lafa þin heafod mid, do swa oft swa þa þearf sy.

Against fainting: take rue and sage and fennel and ground ivy, betony and lily; pound all these herbs together; put into one bag; steep with water; rub well, let it drip out into a vat; take the liquid and warm it and rinse the head with it; do likewise as often as may be needful.

A remedy for insomnia

Slæpdrænc, rædic, hymlic, wermod, belone, cnuca ealle þa wyrte, do in ealað, læt standan ane niht, drince ðonne.

A sleeping drink: radish, hemlock, wormwood, henbane; pound all the plants; put them into ale; let it stand for one night; let him drink it then.

To cure a fever

Wið gedrif, nim snægl ond afeorma hine ond nim þæt clæn fam, menge wið wifes meolc, syle þicgan, him bið sel.

Against a fever: take a snail and cleanse it and take the clean lather and mix with a woman's milk; give it to drink; better will soon come to him.

To cure sea-sickness

Wið wæterseocnysse genim þas wyrte þe man bulbiscillitici ond oðrum naman glædene nemneð ond gedryge hy syððan eal onbutan, genim þonne innewearde, seoð on wætere, ðonne hyt wearm sy seocnys beon ut atogen þærh migðan.

For water-sickness take this plant which one calls 'bulbiscillitici' and by another name 'gladden' and dry it all outwardly afterwards, then take the inside, boil in water, when it is warm mix thereto also honey and vinegar, give three draughts full, very quickly will the sickness be drawn out through the urine.

For spleen pain

Wið miltan sare genim þas wyrte ðe man bryonia ond oþrum naman hymele nemneð, syle þycgean gemang mete, þonne sceal þæt sar lipelice þurh þone micgþan forð gan; ðes wyrt is to þam herigindlic þæt hy man wið gewune drenceas gemencgeað.

For pain of the spleen, take this plant which calls 'bryonia' and by another name 'hop', give it to eat in his food, then the pain must pass mildly out through the urine; this plant is so worthy of praise that it is customarily mixed in potions.

To protect against painful gums

Wið þæra gomena sare gyf hwa þysse wyrte wyrttruman þe man crision ond oðrum naman clæfre nemneð mid him hafað ond on his swyran byrð, næfre him his goman ne deriað.

For pain of the gums, if anyone has with him the root of this plant which one calls 'crision' and by another name 'clover' and carries it on his neck, his gums will never hurt him.

For a spider bite

Wiþ gongewifran bite nim heene æg, gnid on ealu hreaw ond sceapes tord niwe swa he nyte, sele him drincan godne scenc fulne.

For a spider's bite take a hen's egg, crush it raw into ale and fresh sheep's dung, so that he does not know, give him a good cupful to drink.

An anti-inflammatory tonic

Drænc wið ðeore, nim ðas wyrte neoðowearde, ceasteræsc, ontre, ðas ufonwearde betonican, rude, wermod, acremonia, felterre, wuduþistel, feferfuge, æþelferðingcwyrt, ofgeot mid ealað, læt stondan ane niht, drince viiii morgenas lytle bollan fulle swiðe ær ond ete sealtne mete ond nowiht fersces.

A drink against inflammation: take the lower part of these plants: black hellebore, radish: the upper part of these: betony, rue, wormwood, agrimony, felter, wood thistle, feverfew, athelfarthingwort; soak in ale, let it stand for one night; let him drink a small bowlful very early for nine mornings, and let him eat salted food and nothing fresh.

How to compel herbs to reveal their nature

Today we are extremely fortunate to have at our disposal a myriad of different books and volumes packed full of herbal correspondences. We have at our fingertips hundreds of spells for different types of healing situation, and tables of further correspondences which indicate the best time or day to pick the herb, and the most propitious aspect of the lunar cycle with which to perform the accompanying ritual and so on.

I would greatly recommend Ann Moura's book *Green Witchcraft: Folk Magic, Fairy Lore & Herb Craft* for an extensive and well researched account of herbal correspondences and treatments. When constructing a healing spell I always begin by burrowing into my large collection of books and making copious notes. However, such research is only the beginning and forms nothing more than a guide for the construction of the magical ritual, we need to do more than follow a recipe from a book.

It is true that today we can find every piece of factual information we need for spells within books and also of course, from the guidance and support of other Witches, Magicians and Pagan friends. Such ease of information comes at a price however, and that price is the experience of a living and magical relationship with the craft-working, a relationship which empowers the spell beyond normal parameters and compels all the ingredients including our own participation, to reveal and utilise their true nature as it emerges in its fullest potential from the Otherworld.

We may enrich our workings with vitality by making some simple changes, although I do realise that many of you will be doing this quite naturally already. If we remember that everything is alive, interconnected and encompassed by the Otherworld, then even the language we use becomes important and potent. Wherever possible, write your own invocations. Create your poetry with passion and fire of spirit; allow the words to fly high. I often write nothing down before I begin a ritual, allowing the words to flow spontaneously from the Otherworld when the moment arises. This brings an immediate and extremely powerful connection into play which animates our work and makes alive our intentions.

Central to this vital connection is our relationship with the herbs we are using. We may know intellectually what the healing nature of a certain herb should be. Hops for example are widely known to promote sleep and are therefore good to use within a spell for insomnia. However, although performing a spell may certainly have effects due to the natural power of the herb, making magic to create a lasting and powerful change is an entirely different matter indeed.

The following exercise is adapted from a meditation which was recommended by the mystic and philosopher Rudolf Steiner, although I'm sure he adapted it from original shamanic sources. Steiner recognised that we have lost our relationship with the spirit of the natural world, a spirit which we should be in harmony with. The meditation was aimed to re-integrate us with the essential nature of plants and through this relationship, to compel them to reveal their hidden nature to us.

Meditation exercise

You will need to find a plant which is preferably over one year old. It may be a pot plant, a shrub, a small tree, anything which feels right to you. You will also need to have access to the plant for ten minutes every day, from the new to the full moon, and to have some plain paper and coloured pencils to hand.

On the first day of the new moon, find ten minutes to be alone and quiet with your plant. Relax with it and let your thinking mind take a back seat. Notice its leaves or flowers, and let your eyes continue to notice all the tiny parts of the plant. The veins of the leaves, the point where leaf joins stem, the new growth where it emerged from last year's growth and so on. Use your paper and pencils to draw these small parts of the plant, from the newest tips to the oldest stems, and then even down to the seed which is no longer visible beneath the earth. It doesn't matter if you can or can't draw. Your picture may look nothing like the plant; it's the process of attention which matters here. You may draw the newest part of the plant on the first day and the next parts the following day, don't feel you have to draw it all in the first ten minutes.

When you feel you are connecting with your plant, you may cease drawing it and begin using your imagination. Take your mind into the newest tips of the plant, how does it feel in there? Move along the veins of the leaves, feel the energy of growth, feel where the energy is coming from.

The next day move into the growth from last year, sensing the energy of the plant from the inside and feel how last year's growth is different from the newest shoots or growth of the present year. Continue similarly, moving back through time into the oldest sections of the plant until you reach right back to when the plant was just a seed, full of the potential of which you see and feel today. Be that seed for a while. How does it feel?

Now grow outward again, through the stages until you are in the newest tips once more. You can carry out this process over a few days or in one session, whatever feels right for you. You may wish to repeat aspects of it too.

Write down at the end of each session how you feel and what happened. Try to make the sessions culminate at the full moon but do not be too worried about time. If you are not ready to finish then just continue past the full moon noticing how the energy may feel different. If you finish early you might like to meditate with the plant on the full moon when the time comes, and notice how you and the plant feel.

I would recommend repeating this exercise with different plants on a regular basis to develop an intimacy of communication and relationship. When you feel proficient at working in this way with plants and herbs, then you are ready to take the process a subtle step further.

On the next full moon, go back to your original plant and repeat the journey of going back and forward within its growth cycle. When you feel deeply connected, allow your energy to really merge with the plant and then actually *become* the plant. What is your nature? What are your healing properties? Just note down afterwards the answers to your questions, you can always check your responses later with a good plant/herbal guide. This is how the plant will be compelled to reveal its nature, it does so when you realise that you *are* the plant and its nature is your own.

3. DIVINATION AND PROPHECY

'As waters flow over certain places, so the soul penetrates the body and is more noble than it. Even when our external eyes are closed, the soul often sees the future by means of its prophetic powers because it already knows it can live without the body.'

The above quotation from Hildegard of Bingen beautifully captures the essence of divination. Divination is a 'seeing' or 'knowing' of the soul which flows like water from the Otherworld reminding us that true knowledge, especially that of the future, cannot be grasped by our physical endeavours and abilities alone. The soul knows it is immortal, infinite and glorious. It knows too that our human constructs such as space and time, which we use to negotiate our physical reality, can hinder our brilliance and limit our potential. The soul can and does see the future, although it often watches with great sympathy and some amusement, our flailing attempts to employ our mind with its cognitive faculties for predictive purposes.

This chapter will explore the vast and often confusing topic of divination and prophecy in all its manifestations. From the most common forms of cognitive prediction studied by psychologists, to the mysterious non-cognitive immediacy of shamanic seership, I will delve the depths of this captivating ocean.

Psychologists today are increasingly interested in our predictive capabilities. Many experimental projects are being designed right now to better identify how our mind and our mental states evaluate and predict our physical world. Behavioural and social psychologists have found that we humans use a myriad of complex societal predictive strategies, including remarkable skills of observation, evaluation and judgment employed to predict the behaviours of others. For example, I have become an expert at predicting both my cat and husband's behaviours. If I do not feed my cat at five o'clock in the evening, I already know she will give me the cold shoulder for the following hour (at least!) If I were to attempt to feed my husband at five in the evening however, I predict he will not be there to eat the meal. These may appear small and jovial instances of prediction, but the truth is that we are always evaluating our world in this way. Social and evolutionary psychologists argue that we developed this capacity to evaluate a wide amount of physical data and predict certain outcomes, in order to make what appears to be an uncontrollable and hostile world into a safer and more secure place to be. We aim to control the uncontrollable, however; this constant cognitive assessment of our environment is just the tip of a very large iceberg.

There are many terms which are used to identify divinatory practices, and it is necessary to pause here and make some distinctions. Divination is commonly understood to be an interpretative activity using a tool such as tarot cards, runes or the positions of planets in the heavens, to tell the future condition of the person asking for the reading. Prophecy is commonly thought to be a rather different ability which involves communing with a higher consciousness to provide general insights into the human condition. However, such distinctions cloud and confuse the underlying shamanic process which is occurring here.

Whether using cards or a more direct communication, each method is concerned with accessing the flow of knowledge from the Otherworld, they simply differ in the immediacy of contact and relationship. The knowledge of the prophet can be utilised to speak of the future just as readily as that of the tarot reader and therefore, I regard these two categories of diviner and prophet to be referring to the same type of activity, with only the intimacy of engagement with the Otherworld differing.

I propose therefore, a new way of approaching human predictive methods by viewing these activities upon a continuum of fluid boundaries, rather than distinct categories (see the table overleaf). The continuum can be visualised as a line stretching from left to right. The far left indicates our normal cognitive type of predictive strategies investigated by the psychologists. If we move along the line a little towards the right we come to the diviners who use tools such as the runes, a little further brings us to the prophets who engage with the knowledge more directly and at the far end, on the right we have a method of complete immersion within the energies of the Otherworld which was achieved by the ancient seers.

The seer does not just contact the other realm; like the shaman she swims its waters experiencing its mysteries firsthand. Often she cannot verbalise her experiences, as the Otherworld is a pre-cognitive primordial place and thus she would often employ a prophet to interpret her utterances and visions into the every-day cognitive language which others could understand.

The continuum thus spans from the everyday person going about their daily lives dominated by cognition, to the seer who has left the cognitive world behind her entirely. Furthermore, the imagination becomes increasingly dominant as the continuum progresses from the everyday cognitive consciousness, through to the more direct communications of the prophet. However, when we come to the seer, even imagination becomes useless and retreats from the seer, as she moves beyond all boundaries and structures into a divine world.

cognisant	diviner	prophet	seer
Little contact with Otherworld.	Indirect contact with Otherworld through the use of tools.	Direct contact with Otherworld through symbols and signs.	Direct immersion in Otherworld.
Uses cognitive faculties such as judgment, observation and evaluation. Little imagination.	Some use of imagination within the interpretations of the tool and good ability to communicate these interpretations cognitively.	Uses imagination as mediator with some ability to formulate into cognitive language.	Pre-cognitive experience without the need for imaginal mediation.
The experience is often frustrating.	The experience is rewarding.	The experience is uplifting.	The experience is trans-formational. She becomes 'divinised'.
The knowledge produced is limited and hap-hazard.	The knowledge is often reliable but suffers from personal contamination such as opinion and assumption.	Knowledge is very reliable.	The knowledge produced is wholly reliable.

It is the divinatory techniques of the second column which are most prevalent today. Psychic fairs travel the country offering tarot readings whilst astrology and cosmology have been taught within our most enlightened and progressive universities. Furthermore, the rise of psychoanalysis has helped these divinatory practices to find a home in this rather inhospitable scientific world. When Freud began discussing subconscious instincts and Jung began mapping out the archetypes of the unconscious, tarot readers and interpretative diviners became allied to a valid cosmology of psychoanalysis within which, their symbols and signs could be welcomed with some meagre authority.

The study and exploration of symbolism and myth has flourished in recent years too, although mainly as an historic endeavour. The actual process of divination however, the relationship with something 'other' than this physical world, remains eschewed by mainstream society in general. Nonetheless, there is a wealth of information available on all aspects of interpretative divination and I would highly recommend Rachel Pollack's *Seventy Eight Degrees of Wisdom* as a resource for the tarot, and Celeste Teal's *Predicting Events with Astrology* which is good for beginner and intermediate astrologers alike.

It is not my intention to continue where these wonderful authors have already been. I will now focus predominantly upon the two higher types of divination experienced by the prophet and seer, as it is this more direct relational contact with the Otherworld which has been forgotten more than any other in our post-modern world.

The most vivid and detailed account of direct divination from the dark ages, can be found within the Icelandic saga *Erik the Red*. Although the report is situated in Greenland, anthropologists and historians believe this type of practice to have been common throughout Europe and the British Isles. The date of the account is around 930AD or perhaps even earlier, and tells of a time of great hardship and famine in the frozen North where winter conditions had proved even more severe than normal with many villages reaching to the edge of starvation and despair. A Chief Yeoman named Thorkel sought to discover when this time of hardship would finally cease, and to this end he invited a seeress of great renown to visit his people during the winter festival.

Her name was Thorbiorg, although she was also known as Little Sibyl. Thorbiorg was the last surviving sister of nine wicce seers who would travel the lands bringing wisdom and future-telling from the Otherworld. Her description within the saga is hauntingly vivid.

She arrives at the great hall of the village during the evening, cloaked against the cold in deep blue with gems glistening along the seams right to the very ground. Her hood is of black lamb's skin and lined with white cat's fur, and in her hand she wields a great staff with precious gems set into the top. Each hand is clothed in an exquisite white cat skin glove and on her feet she wears calf skin boots with large brass buttons. Around her waist is a girdle made of touch-wood, from which hangs a large leather pouch containing the materials for charms and spell-workings.

Her attire is testimony to her status, indicating that the wicce of old were not always akin to our much loved stereotype of the local wise woman, living in a secluded hovel on the outskirts of the village mixing her potions and living from the land.

The villagers treated Thorbiorg like a Goddess, and it is interesting to note that the great Roman historian Tacitus (AD 56-117), who travelled Northern Europe and the British Isles with the Roman armies recording with intricate detail all the folk customs of its peoples, wrote whilst in Germania of the reverence afforded to certain powerful women called *burgrune* (seers). These powerful women held a place of great honour and authority in society and '*according to the ancient German custom which regards many women as endowed with prophetic powers, and as the superstition grows, attributes divinity to them*'.

In England these women were the *seithr* (seers) and were also exclusively female. It is told that the *seithr* were responsible for teaching Odin the gift of prophesy when he journeyed into the Otherworld by hanging up-side down on the world tree.

Commanding such high social status, Thorbiorg was thus treated to a grand feast of meat, goat's cheese and the hearts of beasts despite the scarcity of food. She was invited to sit upon a throne where she was greeted and welcomed with salutations, and Thorkel asked her to cast her eyes about his home and his people to see their worthiness. Thorbiorg responded that she was very pleased with the character of the people and that after a night's sleep, she would help the village by answering their questions regarding the future.

The following day Thorbiorg began the preparations for her ritual which would serve to enable her seeing of the future. She called for the villagers to bring any local wicce able to make spell-workings to assist her with the necessary incantations. Unfortunately none could be found and so:

'Thereupon a search was made throughout the house, to see whether anyone knew how to recite the [incantation]. Then the girl Gudrid said: "Although I am neither skilled in the magic arts nor a sibyl, yet my foster-mother, Halldis, taught me in Iceland that spell-song, which she called Warlocks." Thorbiorg answered: "Then thou art wise in season!" Gudrid replied: "This is an incantation and ceremony of such a kind, that I do not intend to lend it any aid, for I am a good Christian woman." Thorbiorg answered: "It could so be that thou couldst give thy help to the people here, yet still be a good Christian woman; but I will leave it with Thorkel to provide for my needs."

Thorkel orders Gudrid to assist Thorbiorg with the special incantation and the ritual commences with the women of the village forming a circle with Thorbiorg at the centre, whilst Gudrid sings the incantation so beautifully that it enchants all who have gathered there. Thorbiorg thanks Gudrid for her singing saying:

"She has indeed lured many spirits here who have found the song to be very pleasant to hear; those spirits who wanted to forsake us and refuse to submit themselves to us have joined us here. Many

things are now revealed to me which were previously hidden, both, from me and from others. I am able to proclaim that this period of famine will not endure and the fortunes will increase as spring approaches. The visitation of disease, which has been so long upon you, will disappear sooner than expected. And thee, Gudrid, I shall reward for your assistance as your destiny has also been revealed to me. Thou shalt make a most worthy marriage here in Greenland, but it shall not be of long duration for your future path leads out to Iceland, and a lineage both great and goodly shall spring from thee, and above thy line brighter rays of light shall shine than I have power clearly to reveal. And now farewell and health to thee, my daughter!"

Following this general assurance that the evil and difficult times would pass, Thorbiorg welcomed individuals from the village to come up to her and ask their private concerns. It is told that little of what she prophesied failed to come to pass and after the ritual was finished, the great seeress continued her journey through the frozen North to attend further invitations.

There are other surviving records from all over Europe of more great seers with the gift of direct inspirational prophesising of the future. Tacitus also writes in his Germania chronicles that the tribes *'believe that there resides in women an element of holiness and a gift of prophecy'* and he puts forward the example of Valeda, a great Germanic seeress whom the Romans encountered during their defeat of 69AD.

Unusually, the Romans had been forced by the revolting German tribes to attempt a peaceful negotiation. They were shocked however; to be informed that such a negotiation would have to be conducted with Valeda. Valeda was a seer of Germania who had prophesied the Roman defeat and it was she who held tribal authority. She was revered and respected and far too sacred to be seen by any other than her attendants who were skilled at the interpretation of her visions and utterances, and it was through the mediation of these men that all negotiations with the Romans were conducted.

The role of the seer does not emerge only from the Northern territories of what is now Europe and Scandinavia, but can also be found with striking similarity within the classical world. The Greeks and Romans also viewed women as having a mysterious yet privileged access to a type of knowledge forgotten by the wider world.

Seers were termed *manteis* and the *manteis* would experience visions and ecstasies in which new knowledge would emerge to enrich and illuminate our embodied consciousness. However, their visionary reports were often difficult to decipher, and so they would have special attendants called *prophetai* who would interpret their utterances for people to understand. We have here a clear example of the two upper columns of the continuum.

There is a direct experiential meeting with the Otherworld which appears to occur in a visionary and pre-cognitive state and an interpretative form of divination where the *prophetai* will interpret the utterances and symbols which have emerged into our world through the *manteis,* and present this information in normal cognitive linguistic terms. Cosmologically this makes sense.

As was mentioned in chapter one, the Otherworld is a pre-condition for our own and it follows therefore, that it necessarily pre-dates our human cognitive faculty. Those prophesising directly from the Otherworld would find difficulty in presenting their experiences in a form which our cognitive level of consciousness can apprehend.

Unfortunately, with the rise of reason and rationality during the Enlightenment combined with the earlier rise of Christianity, the balanced relationship between the *manteis* and *prophetai* and thus between knowledge of the Otherworld and knowledge of our own, disintegrated. Seers became figures viewed with suspicion, figures to be reviled and to be feared. As 'real' and 'true' knowledge became the auspices of men, particularly priests and scholars, women's sacred gifts were derided and categorised as irrational and evil. Women had picked the fruits of the Otherworld and brought back their diabolical knowledge to infect our physical realm. Therefore, the seer and the witch presented a fearsome, irrational, ritualistic and overtly female road to knowledge, embodying what Plato termed a *divine frenzy* which requires an apparent loss of control akin to madness. Indeed visionary states of ecstasy must have seemed almost identical to madness when observed. As the 12th century writer known as Gerald of Wales describes:

'they immediately go into a trance and lose control of their senses, as if they are possessed. They do not answer the question put to them in a logical way. Words stream from their mouths, incoherently and apparently meaningless and without any sense at all, but all the same well expressed: and if you listen carefully to what they say you will receive the solution to your problem. When it is all over, they will recover from their trance, as if they were ordinary people waking from heavy sleep.'

The mystic philosopher Socrates once stated however, that '*our greatest blessings come to us by way of madness.'* Socrates understood that true knowledge which stands and speaks beyond the confines of time requires not just a cognitive faculty to decipher meaning within our thinking world, but also the ability to 'lose the mind' to enable such knowledge to emerge in the first place. Therefore, this ecstatic form of primordial divinatory knowledge truly is the most fundamental and important form of knowing upon which, every aspect of human understanding grows and forms.

This is an ancient realisation which if remembered today, would have immense implications for our modern methods of education, enquiry and engagement with life. Direct divination has become all but extinct today because we are so reliant upon cognitive interpretative skills which I would argue, are indeed mere shadows of our full capabilities regarding the process of understanding ourselves and our world.

However, the 'mainstream' world has been abundant with great and authoritative thinkers and philosophers who have understood the importance of this pre-linguistic and pre-cognitive 'knowing'. The great philosopher Immanuel Kant argued for example, that real genius of the type that brings forth new world changing ideas and inventions, requires a transcendental awareness beyond the limitations of the mundane physical world. Without this first seed of inspirational contact with the transcendental realm, a realm we now understand to be the Otherworld, thought and the production of thought is inert and without meaning. Inspired thought however, is an activity of the soul which bursts with true enlightenment bringing meaning to the mundane, and when meaning flows unhindered from the Otherworld into this, life is fully lived, experienced and more importantly, transformed.

The direct divinations of Thorbiorg did not go so far into the Otherworld that all semblance of sanity appeared lost however. She was able to report with great coherence the knowledge which was revealed to her reminding us that divinatory skill exists along the continuum rather than being cast into categories. Thorbiorg still retained a connection within the mundane world, a connection she was careful to construct and maintain by utilising ritual and ritual space such as the circle. Having secured this contact with the physical world, Thorbiorg then established her connection with the divine using the required incantations and spell-workings.

Thorbiorg's divinatory work is most akin therefore, to the shamanic divinations of the wicce and other pre-modern peoples around the globe who stood with a foot in both this and the Otherworld, by engaging in both structural ritual support and divine communication. Surviving reports of complete immersion into the Otherworld however, are unfortunately scarce. To find written evidence we must turn to the middle ages which nonetheless, often retain the continuity of consciousness experienced by our wicce ancestors. Perhaps surprisingly, those reports which do survive concern the ecstasies and divine frenzies of Nuns, sisters of the Catholic Church. Such remarkable and mystical women walked a difficult path however, as their prophetic visions were viewed either as witchery inspired by the devil, or as the mark of a future saint in the making, depending upon the time and area in which they lived.

One of the few surviving accounts of this rare inspirational divinatory practice and experience was written in the sixteenth century by Saint Teresa of Avila.

Teresa was born in 1515 to a Christian family within a very Christian community. A sickly child, she was often cared for by the church and specifically the sisters of her local convent. Her gifts of visions and prophetic ecstasies emerged over time and caused both Teresa and the church great concern. One way in which Teresa sought to come to terms with her ecstasies and communicate their relevance to the Church Fathers, was to write a biographical account of her remarkable experiences.

Her collected works was aimed at assuaging the fear and mystery which surrounded such strange occurrences, and when reading the work it becomes apparent that Teresa felt compelled to explain herself to a Church which was scared and suspicious of her strangely womanly power, and one cannot help but feel that had Teresa not established such a close relationship with the Church from such a young age, then she may well have been persecuted by it and victim of a grisly fate.

Teresa's biography is not an easy read for Christian or non-Christian alike. The Christian is challenged by the ecstasies which even today appear more supernatural and 'witchy' than Christian. The non-Christian however, is subjected to a bombardment of the most nauseatingly saccharine tributes to Church and Christ to which Teresa positions herself in painful subordination and lowliness in comparison. Her story contains such conflict between her embodiment of all that Tacitus described as the power and 'being' of the great pagan *burgrune* in direct contrast to the meek and mild God fearing nun who owes all and everything to Christ and the Church. The following will give some insight into her great struggle:

'In the case of a poor little woman like myself, weak and with hardly any fortitude, it seems to me fitting that God lead me with gifts....so that I might be able to suffer some trials. But when I see servants of God, men of prominence, learning, and high intelligence make so much fuss because God doesn't give them devotion, it annoys me to hear them.'

Teresa alludes here to the jealousy of the Clergy who are making a 'fuss' because Teresa, a mere woman has been blessed with God's gifts where they, despite their great scholasticism, have not. We can see how Teresa must have walked a very difficult and careful line as throughout her work, when she has cause to be critical of the Church and its 'men of prominence', she is always at great pains to subordinate herself as a weak powerless woman of no learning, in contrast to the superior position of men and Church.

Within her writing Teresa aims to describe and actually teach others how to be open enough to allow the gifts of God to manifest within us. She states that these visionary gifts cannot be sought out, as they can only be offered to those who have left behind certain egoic vestments. Jealousy she argues is one way of becoming blind and estranged from the potentials of God's gifts, as is desire for power and attitudes of intolerance.

Teresa goes on to describe the process of visionary states of ecstasy and makes the observation that when God delivers an ecstasy upon her, the experience is not necessarily intended to be one which we may *'understand... while on earth; He knows we are incapable of doing so. I have seen this for myself.'* And this is because, when we enter an ecstatic state or 'rapture' then as Teresa describes, God enables a *'suspending of the faculties for a while'* which allows that *'flight is given to the spirit so that it may be elevated...The flight is an easy flight, a delightful one, a flight without noise.'* During these times *'The soul laughs to itself over the time when it esteemed money and coveted it.... [and] It deplores the*

*time in which it was concerned about its reputation and deplores the
deception it suffered in believing that what the world called honour
was honour.'*

We can see how Teresa describes her visionary experiences as
involving a suspension of certain faculties, which she identifies in
her biography as cognitive and sensory faculties. The suspension
of these faculties removes the divinatory experience far from the
mundane physical world, to a point where even interpretation
seems unlikely. This pre-cognitive immersion is wholly obscure
to us however, Teresa's gifts do not always remain quite so
perplexing and sometimes her experience moves into more
cognitive parameters.

Teresa decribes the fluidity of her visions which at times are
indeed formed far beyond the realms of the cognitive or even the
imaginal, fully immersing Teresa in the Otherworld, yet other
times her visions do enter the auspices of her imaginative faculty.
She explains how the images revealed from the Otherworld, or
from God as Teresa would say, are *'not like an earthly drawing
no matter how perfect it may be.'* She goes on to clarify how the
images which come to her are not dead like a painting of a person
for example, but rather, the images are very much alive depicting
real people and events from the Otherworld. The more intense
the rapture however, the more *'imageless'* the experience and
'an imageless way is more perfect.' Teresa explains that an intense
rapture can only be experienced, not thought, as it exists even
beyond the *'eyes of the soul'*, it is indeed a primordial experience of
pure truth and pure love. It is the experience of the divinised seer.

Teresa labours over these explanations and descriptions,
knowing she is trying to conjure an understanding for her reader
which is only truly comprehended from actual experience, rather
than inadequate words. She elaborates further therefore upon the
fluidity of the boundaries of divinatory experience, explaining that
the more symbolic prophetic experience involving imagination
and the wholly non-cognitive raptures beyond the imagination,

can at times occur in tandem. However, the more one moves into the cognitive world, our world, the more one must beware the deceptions of the devil although '*The devil very quickly shows who he is....[and] .. where there is experience, the devil, in my opinion, can do no harm.*' By 'experience' Teresa is referring to an authentic immersion within the Otherworld and if you think back to the exercise in the first chapter, the deceptions of the ego become easier and easier to spot as you continue to develop a real 'experience' by engaging the alchemical imagination.

It is important to note however, that the ego's whims and desires are not 'bad' as long as they are not confused with real work within the Otherworld. We are encouraged with a new dogma today to 'conquer' the ego which is a mostly futile endeavour, which thus causes us an underlying anxiety combined with a constant sense of failure. If the ego wishes to adventure and tell you wild stories then listen with amusement as you would to the stories of a small and excited child, and just like the child, the ego will move on swiftly enough to the next delight and wonder. Just know that it is a story full of fancy and desire, which you have the ability to either give your energy to so the stories manifest, or not.

All you need to do is to be able to recognise when the images and fantasies in your mind are ego constructions or actual energetic flowings from the Otherworld. Then you can decide which you will simply enjoy and let go of, and which you will focus your intent upon to bring into manifestation. It is your choice and your results. The ego is not the devil and it is not negative or bad, this is a Christianised distinction.

After describing the nature and actual experience of direct divination, Teresa goes on to explain the consequence of such experiences to be an amazing transformation of the body and soul:

'*One cannot exaggerate the richness that the true vision leaves; it even gives health to the body and leaves it comforted.*'

Swimming in the waters on the Otherworld is thus a

transformative experience on all levels. The shamanic wicce did not only plunge its depths to be of service to others in need, but also to grow and develop as spiritual immortal beings themselves. Immersion within the Otherworld, a realm of divine energy can cause us to become 'divinised' and healed by the experience.

This reminds me of an article I once read by Mellen-Thomas Benedict who recounted an extraordinary near death experience after dying from terminal cancer. He was dead for an hour and a half and during this time, he describes journeying through the universe with spirit guides who revealed to him many truths. He recalls being washed by the flowing spiritual essence of the spark of creation itself, the divine energy which was healing and renewing. Miraculously, he was able to choose to return to his body, even though he had been gone for a long time and when he awoke in his hospital bed with the sheet pulled up over his head, he was cured of all cancer.

Immersion into the Otherworld by death or ecstasies leads to a profound healing where the diviner or seer becomes 'divinised', washed by the very creative primordial flowing which exists beyond physical illness or death. By developing such abilities we too can become healed and transformed.

Jung saw this divinised state as the culmination of his psychoanalytic process of individuation, where the patient would engage their alchemical imagination to re-integrate the different aspects of self such as the shadow, anima and animus into a whole unified being. The recent long awaited publication of Jung's own personal journal *The Red Book*, which presents his shamanic questing into the imaginal realm, is quite amazing. However, Teresa teaches that the ultimate experience of becoming 'divinised' lay beyond the soul, beyond the imagination and beyond the mind. It occurs within a space, if we can even call it a space, where only immanent experience appears to exist. Perhaps the closest thing we have to comprehending this ineffability is love.

Few ancient or historic reports of direct divinatory experience exist beyond those already recounted here. There are some reports of divination being conducted although it is impossible to be sure what type is being talked about. In England, sources are scarce although in the infamous and colourful trial of Eleanor Duchess of Gloucester in 1441, who was charged with treasonable witchcraft, enough documentation survives to offer us some clues. Eleanor was accused of having employed the use of divination to predict the King's death, and of using magic to ensure the succession of her husband to the royal throne. Eleanor was a keen occultist and had called upon the services of a well known witch of the time called Margery Jourdemayne, to advise and assist her magical endeavours. It was said of Eleanor:

> 'How she in waxe by counsel of the witch,
> An image made, crowned like a King,
> ....which dayly they did pytch
> Against a fyre, that as the wax did melt,
> So should his lyfe consume away unfelt.'

The use of image magic may indicate that Eleanor's divinations fortold of ill fortune for her ambitions, and thus she required the above magical intervention to ensure her husband's future royal role. However, Eleanor's husband died in mysterious circumstances and Margery was burnt for witchcraft. We will never know what type of divinatory technique was employed but perhaps it could be speculated that fate remained consistent despite Eleanor's magical endeavours to the contrary.

The weaving of fate was considered a powerful and mysterious thing by the wicce diviners or *seithr*. Our ancestors believed that three sisters called the Norns sat beneath the world tree, weaving our destinies and the fates of all. The woven web did not exist in linear time however, that is a human invention and therefore, the web contained and embraced the past, present, future and all the worlds. The Norns, also known as the wyrd sisters to denote their skill in destiny weaving, do not just weave the fates of human kind but also, they created and thus weaved the fates of the Gods too. If we delve a little deeper we can see therefore, that these three women, so evocative of the Trinitarian aspects of the Goddess and the later Christian God, created reality, and if we wish to divine knowledge of the future we must look to the present moment which is the only moment which exists and therefore, the only moment to include all others which were, which are and which are to come.

Eckhart Tolle has famously termed this moment *The Power of Now*, and it is this moment into which the seer swims and returns with her apparently 'mad' uttering from a world where no material constructs exist.

Developing the skill of direct divination

I have had the great fortune to have experienced some amazing tarot readings although I do not feel that any method of divination is actually superior to any other, as all emerge from the flowing of Otherworldly knowledge with some practitioners preferring to interpret the signs and symbols which this flowing manifests, whilst others prefer to engage the energy directly. It could certainly be argued that the former is far more useful to us, we are after all, cognitive beings living within the physical realm and what use are the abstract, confusing utterances of seers for us today?

It is uncommon to find contemporary examples of direct divination although I do remember receiving a particularly accurate tarot reading once from a psychic who combined her interpretation of the cards, with a visionary skill. Although the actual tarot reading was extremely good, it was the direct inspirational visions she relayed to me which turned out to be startlingly accurate as they manifested. Before she had turned even one card, she looked at me with an intent gaze and told me that I was clawing my way out of a dark pit of despair. I certainly was!

I was in my early twenties, just setting my first tentative footfalls into the big wide world when I fell head over heels for one of my tutors who unbeknownst to me, was a serial love rat who preyed upon women far younger than himself, bleeding them dry financially. By the time I realised what was truly happening I was in a terrible situation, and with no family to help me I descended into a darkness which seemed so overwhelming I stared death in the face more than once. I relay this to emphasise how amazing the tarot reader's predictions were to me, as she foretold through her visions, of a beautiful house in my future where I would be able to pursue my dreams and be happy. Thanks to my husband, that future became real for me although given my situation all those years ago, the prediction seemed preposterous and extremely cruel.

A further experience happened to me in a spiritualist church. For anyone who has not attended a spiritualist meeting let me explain. Most meetings are Christian in sentiment, with a congregation singing hymns and saying prayers as one does in church. Half way through the service, instead of the communion of the Eucharist, there is a communion with spirit. A medium will take the platform and lead the people with an inspirational prayer after delivering a suitable spiritual reading. Then follows the communion, where the medium will come to individuals within the congregation with messages for them from loved ones who have passed over into spirit.

The quality of mediums today is quite appalling as spiritual churches readily admit. Many apparent mediums have not been able to differentiate ego cravings from true soul work, and the confused result is often painful and embarrassing to watch. Occasionally however, real spirit sings.

I remember sitting through a service at the Tunbridge Wells Spiritualist Church in England. The medium who took the service did not attempt to preen and brag or 'perform' with the forced sincerity so often apparent and interestingly, most of her information was visionary rather than coming from the spirits of the dead. When she came to me she said that she had an image of me holding up some kind of coloured crystal to the light. I was apparently taking different colours of this crystal type thing and holding these colours up to the light in turn. I had no idea what she was talking about.

Five years later, I suddenly caught myself doing exactly what she had described. I had taken a course in stained glass making and really enjoyed it. One afternoon, having bought some of my own equipment for my home including a large amount of small glass samples, I needed to find just the right shade of blue and gold glasses and there I was, holding each colour up to the light in turn.

Both of the above examples illustrate how different types of diviner can move along the continuum unbound by categorical conventions. My tarot reader used cards whilst the medium used contact with the dead, yet both also drew upon their skills of direct visionary inspiration and it was this fleeting but powerful ability that yielded the most accurate and memorable results. The results may not have been particularly world shattering, there were no mystical revelations or life changing miracles to speak of and I have no doubt many of you have had far greater experiences.

However, the constant flowing of knowledge from the Otherworld does not judge what is relevant or not relevant, the flowing simply flows. Everything is there, from the brand of toothpaste I buy in the shops tomorrow to the fate of the human race, it is the skill of the diviner to swim the currents and encourage the required answers to come forward from the myriad of potential snippets of information. My tarot reader may have had a little more skill than the medium as she did draw upon knowledge which related directly to my concerns, even if I did not believe a word of it at the time.

Great diviners such as Thorbiorg were able to access very specific threads within the wyrd sister's woven universe to answer the community's questions. It is skill, experience and courage therefore, which enables the wicce to swim the waters of the Otherworld and return with what they require, and it is this skill that the following exercise and ritual begins to develop.

Scrying as a mode of divination

Scrying involves using a reflective or luminescent surface such as water, mirror, crystal or even fire and allowing this material to serve as a medium for Otherworldly visions or insights. Although we may not realise that we are doing it, many of us scry on a regular basis. I often find myself cloud gazing, sliding from the mundane world into a trance like state where the thinking mind wanders off for a while, content in its own distractions allowing me to open my inner eyes and *see*. It is exhilarating to just let things flow, morph, and see what morsels come forward. Perhaps an issue that has been causing me concern suddenly springs into focus and takes on a new light of resolution, or maybe I simply find a moment of wisdom and peace within a hectic day. The point is that scrying enables us to grow closer to the Otherworld and bathe in its watery currents. The watery metaphor is extremely apt, and it is unsurprising that the most popular scrying tool is, and always has been, water.

Ancient reminders of the powerful qualities of water exist in many place names. For example, in England there is a sweet little village called Fritwell in Oxfordshire which is a combination of the Anglo-Saxon (OE) words *freht* (augury/diviner) and *well* (spring). I don't know whether Fritwell retains its original sacred spring, but we may assume the spring was regarded for its divinatory properties where the energy from the Otherworld was perhaps strong, flowing as water from within the earth. Water was therefore a symbolic reflection of the 'flowing' of Otherworldly knowledge, a flowing which was constant and pure and which can come to us freely if we approach it in the right way.

Water scrying (hydromancy) also serves to remind us that images and reflections are very real indeed. Today we often feel conflicted regarding images. Marketing companies use images to wield extraordinary power over almost every aspect of our lives. We are manipulated sometimes subtly most often overtly into buying certain products or adopting popular values. Everyone seems to be selling something with an image be it a product, a public figure, an election, a religion or a life style and we are seduced and obsessed by images like moths to a light. Furthermore, we are constantly comparing ourselves to the images we see. Is our figure or our face like hers, is my house as beige as the one in the glossy magazine? New-age gurus respond with a reactionary call to arms telling us that this image worship is unhealthy and it is distracting us from the reality of the spiritual path and must be eschewed. Modern Gnosticism also supports the notion that this world full of images is a false illusion, an evil of egoic deception and we must strive against it to rid ourselves of shadows.

The shamanic wicce had a rather different view. The physical world with its images is not evil; it is sacred to the Mother Goddess who bore it. We are the Earth and it is us. Images are not the problem; it is our severance of the umbilical cord which has cast us into confusion, left us malnourished and unable to distinguish between worlds.

The great philosopher Heidegger argued that images and appearances are not deceiving. Images are real messages from the Otherworld and as Heidegger's contemporary Roberts Avens suggests, even '*the soul is image*'. This means that we do not just live in an animated universe where the rocks and trees are alive, everything is alive! Blake even went so far as to say that images, imagination and their manifestations '*is human Existence itself*'.

This means that images and visions which come to you within the following scrying ritual are real, they are you, they are within you and without you and when you swim within the existence which is everything, *you* are reborn moment by moment. We do not scry, we *are* the scrying and Avens also says, the only way to truly swim in this energy of *being* which is *you*, is by holding it in the heart, not the head.

We do not begin the process of developing our scrying by seeking answers, although many books insist you start with a question in mind. We begin by allowing the flowing to come to us in the same way springs bubble up from the earth and in the same way dreams come to us, from beyond ourselves. The wicce had a saying, *mec gemœtte* which means 'to me came a dream' rather than 'I had a dream' which we say today. We seem to think that dreams and visions are ours, that they are things which happen to us yet this is not the case. We are embraced by the Otherworld and its energies which flow to us. We just need to recognise and experience this flowing and only then can we attempt to swim in a direction with a specific question in mind. If we try to swim too soon, then our thinking mind will highjack the whole experience.

The first ritual I present (step one) is designed to enable you to experience the flowing of knowledge and gain some visions and inspirations. The wicce would scry upon certain days, when the veil between this and the spiritual world was felt to be at its most permeable.

Witches today continue this custom with the great Samhain celebration at Halloween being an ancient time for scrying and divining. In the past, maidens would often stare into a mirror upon this night with the hope of glimpsing their future husband. If however, they saw the face of a skull, this would indicate that they would die before their marriage. The dark of the moon is also a good time to scry. When the moon is between its waxing and waning its energy becomes sympathetic to introspection and quiet meditative reflections. I would therefore recommend commencing the first stage of the ritual upon one of these times and then practising it for at least a month if possible before moving on to step two.

Step one, ritual

There are many books which give details and exercises in scrying. Cassandra Eason's *Scrying the Secrets of the Future* gives a comprehensive account of different methods and ideas which surround the practice. What follows is my own tried and tested method which requires a large bowl of water, a pen, paper and some black ink. The ink is not absolutely necessary but is preferable. If you wish to cast a circle then you will also need whatever items you normally use. Casting a circle both aids the meditative state and helps to create a sacred space, dedicated and protected from the hustle and bustle of energies swirling around our busy world.

Begin by giving yourself a good thirty minutes of undisturbed time. Have all your items before you including the candles and other tools you usually use to cast your circle if that is what you would like to do. If you are new to circle casting I would recommend following my instructions at the beginning of the ritual where I have kept the casting as simple as possible. Great elaborate invocations and ceremonial ornamentation are not necessary for this ritual but those of you familiar to circle casting may feel free to disregard mine and continue as you wish.

Casting the circle

Facing east, take three deep centring breaths and say *"spirits of the east, ancient elements of air, I ask that you join me here in my circle, I bid you hail and welcome"*. Imagine air in whatever way feels right to you. Really see it there and feel its vital energy of the high intellect. Without air we could never bring our greatest ideas into manifestation.

Facing south say *"spirits of the south, ancient elements of fire, I ask that you join with me in my circle, I bid you hail and welcome"*. Imagine fire in whatever way you please and feel its passion and energy, it is this energy which compels us into action, to make our ideas into reality. Repeat the same process in the west for water/emotion and the north for earth/physical manifestation.

Returning to the east, extend your right arm and imagine a blue light emanating from your fingertips as you turn clockwise around the room, seeing this light creating a circle about you. You may use a magical tool such as a knife or wand for this if you wish. Say *"I cast this circle as a space between worlds and outside of time"*. You may invite the Goddess and God to join your circle too, although it is not always necessary to do this formally as they are always with you anyway.

If you find this casting to be too ritualistic and long, perhaps you would prefer my favourite casting as follows. You need a lantern or candle with lighted flame. Carrying the flame in your right hand, walk slowly, clockwise around the circumference of the space you are dedicating and imagine in your mind's eye the light from the flame remaining as a circular bluish hue. As you walk say *"I carry this flame of light around this sacred place and ask that all spirits depart unless invited. I welcome the great elements of balance to ward this place and I welcome the Goddess our Mother and the great God to join me in these works. All hail!"*

Scrying

Now settle yourself in the centre of your circle and feel the balancing energies of the elements around you. Take your bowl of water and add a few drops of ink watching the ink swirl round and round, creating shapes and patterns. Mix the ink further if needed to create a dark pool. If you wish, you may choose to bless the water before you begin with a pinch of salt. Take your time and meditate a little.

When you feel totally relaxed take some deep breaths and let your eyes gently come to rest on the surface of the water. Try not to strain your eyes, so let them defocus if that is what they want to do. You may notice the swirls of ink, ripples or the reflections of light and other objects from the room. Allow the thinking mind to become disinterested in such things and to float away when it wishes. Sometimes it will return and make comments to you, just let it speak but pay little attention and it will drift again soon enough. The thinking mind just loves our attention and becomes easily bored when we withhold our devotion from it.

Just gaze gently at the water. Images rarely appear with brilliant clarity, although with practice this can occur. Just let images come without pre-judging what you think you should be seeing. It's okay to close the eyes between images if they become heavy. Often I have closed my eyes and entered a deep trance where direct visionary experience has taken over completely. At first though, it can take time to let the thinking mind drift and to trust the images that come. Often, the images are there, but we have our soul eyes closed to them as the thinking mind tells us that nothing of value is really happening. Do not feel disheartened if nothing occurs during your first few sessions.

When you feel it's time to stop, record anything important in your notebook. Put down anything and everything, even any frustrations, distractions or simply the way you feel. Now you can banish the circle. Retrace your earlier steps but this time give thanks to the elements for their help and guidance, and then bid them hail and farewell. With each element, let's take air for example, imagine it dissipating back into the cosmos from where it came, and with the circle use your left, receptive hand to re-absorb the energy. When all is done, it's always good to eat something to bring us firmly back to the physical again.

Interpretation

The best way to interpret your images is by deep personal reflection. If you saw a butterfly for example, you would need to reflect upon what butterflies mean to you, why are they important and how do feel about this particular visitation?

In my own scrying, if something I have seen remains curious and confusing I sometimes work with it over the coming days in my alchemical imagination. I may draw the butterfly and then go into the image in my imagination and ask it why it came to me and what it needs to tell me. Although this type of interaction is always best, I include below a brief list of common scrying symbols and images as a possible guide for interpretation. Remember however, that many images may be very personal to your life and many also have multiple meanings. Saying that, as Jung argued, there is often a commonality to symbols, as if images and symbols are indeed a coherent primordial language in their own right. Use lists of symbolic meanings as guides therefore if you get stuck, but never assume them to be written in stone.

Symbols

Butterfly: Transformation and initiation.

Circles: Unity, eternity, divinity.

Moon: A symbol for the Goddess and gifts of prophecy,. resurrection, intuition, fertility.

Spiral: Expansion of consciousness.

Cross: Represents the meeting of heaven and earth, the connection between this world and the Otherworld.

Sun: Creation, the development of a project or idea, action, doing.

Angel: Soul-searching, harmony, strength, relationship, message.

House: The state of the house and how you feel about it

reflects your current situation.

Owl: wisdom, mystery, secrecy.

Step two, learning to swim

Step one encourages a relationship with Otherworldly knowledge. It is not designed to direct or engage with the energy and that is why I do not ask you to think of a question. It is very important to able to sit quietly and just allow the energy to flow towards you and through you. As soon as we ask a question, we invite the thinking mind to bring all of its baggage and neurosis along. It begins to filter the flowing and may even stop it altogether by over analysing and pre-judging the sorts of images that emerge. The thinking mind worries that perhaps our question should be formulated differently and if only we had thought of this or that instead, then things may be different. Before we know it, doubt and uncertainty have been effectively cast with nothing of any value breaking through the thinking mind's assault-course of hostility.

Only when you feel that you have been able to be and exist within the flowing without the thinking mind high-jacking the experience should you then begin to ask a question. When you feel ready to take this next step, then repeat the ritual as before. This time however, before you begin, create a question. Be very clear about what it is and keep it as straightforward as possible. When you are sure about what it is you wish to ask then take some time to express your question as a symbol. For example, if I wanted to know if I was going to pass an exam I may symbolise this as a book. It need only be a very simple image of a book and I would draw this on a piece of paper. I could equally have drawn something abstract, a squiggle even, it is your own intention that the symbol stands for your question which is important.

Now cast your circle and continue as in step one. When you

come to the scrying, hold the symbol in your mind for a few moments (not the question!) and then let it go from your mind and relax into the scrying as before. If you feel the thinking mind wanting to dominate, just let it say its stuff and let it go, do not engage it or comment on it. I sometimes allow the thoughts to assume the shape of bubbles and watch them drift off into the ether. If the thinking mind is being particularly talkative and overly interested in what you are doing, then you may like to imagine the flowing energy of the Otherworld as a light coming from the water and going to your heart and not your head. This can help. When you are ready to stop then continue as in step one.

Divining with our dreams

A further form of direct divination occurs through dreaming. Some wicce would be particularly skilled in dream premonition and others sought to develop such skills, as they considered the information which flowed from the dark of sleep to be highly reliable. Normally, when we are asleep, our minds run riot with imaginary and often incoherent exertions whilst other times, our minds are simply static, idle. Knowing what we now know concerning the reality of the imagination, the energy it can wield and the effects it can have, we are in a better position to see clearly just how powerful and spirituality profitable dream time can be. I do not use the words 'power' and 'profit' to induce hope of gaining superiority over others but rather, to indicate the extraordinary effects such work may have upon us.

During the waking hours we are assuaged by a myriad of social conformities, judgements and evaluative decision making which limit and hinder our abilities to perceive and act from our true selves. During sleep we have no such limitations. Sleep affords us a unique opportunity within our normally bounded world to break free of constraints for the night. However, we need to be able to move from the normal disordered imaginings we are accustomed to within our dreaming, which waste so much energy, to a clearer more intended experience.

Tonight, as you retire to bed, try the following. Before getting into bed, take a few minutes to wash your hands, feet and face and when you are in bed lay on your right side. Be careful not to let yourself get drawn into the wanderings of the mind, just allow any thoughts to drift through and out, don't hold onto them or get involved. Push any negative thoughts quickly through on their journey, just let them go.

Hold in your mind's eye a pure light. The light is perfectly clear. Hold the light and allow sleep to come. If we move from waking to sleep with a clarity of intent and sight, this energy will continue within our dreaming providing clearer, less cluttered images and understandings. When you awake in the morning always write down your dreams whilst they are fresh. Many who persevere with this exercise begin to experience what are called lucid dreams and actually gain a certain amount to conscious control whilst dreaming. This can lead to very rapid and lasting transformations for a person on all levels.

Before moving on to delve into the compelling world of shapeshifting, you may wonder why a chapter based upon the divinations of the Anglo-Saxon witch fails to contain any reference to rune casting. The casting of the runes was most certainly a very common form of divination for our ancestors in England yet so much has been written and told of this custom it requires little embellishment from me. I would recommend reading Tony Linsell's 'Anglo-Saxon Mythology, Migration and Magic' which I believe is one of the best resources for runic reading. The book is illustrated by Brian Partridge and his art works are arguably the most inspirational representations of the runes available.

4. SHAPESHIFTING

'Human rationality says to each person, 'You are this or that animal'....'

Hildegard of Bingen, *Physica* (1158 c.e).

If you have tried the exercises and meditations from the previous chapters then you have already begun to tread the path of the shapeshifter. Shapeshifting is all about energy, and every time you work with energy you are shifting to some degree.

Absolutely everything is composed of energy, even our emotions, and when you change from being happy to sad or vice versa, you are shifting energy. Shamans often talk of shapeshifting therefore, when they are referring to almost any type of change imaginable however, the term is usually and specifically known to us through its most unimaginable quality, the quality of physically transforming from human into animal form. The material world of physical manifestation is by far the densest energy of all, at least that is how things currently appear to be and unfortunately we are taught, or rather conditioned into believing that this densest from of energy cannot be shifted. If only we were brought up to believe otherwise we would be shapeshifting all the time!

This chapter explores the shifting phenomenon from the modern cinematic manifestations still with us today, back in time to the middle ages, dark ages and pre-historic times. From the palatable and perhaps believable forms of mental and etheric shapeshifting to the altogether bizarre world of physical shifting, we will journey beyond the constructs of normality towards the culmination of the chapter where exercises are presented for anyone who feels curious enough to howl, prance and generally embrace their animal form.

My first experience of shapeshifting occurred whilst I was still quite young. I had always been interested in the occult phenomena of our amazing universe and I remember my Grandfather once saying to me that I had been born with a hunger for the unknown and mysterious, a hunger which would come to dominate my life. He was quite right. I was but seven years old therefore, when I witnessed my first shapeshift.

A family friend called Philip was and still is, a physical medium. Physical mediumship is rare and commonly involves the medium working directly with spirits of the departed through their personal spirit guide which serves to protect the medium, enabling spirits to actually manifest and appear once again in their earthly form by utilising etheric energy. Etheric energy is vibrationally the closest energy to physical matter, and the medium expends this energy which appears as a white semi-material substance called ectoplasm, which the spirit will then use to recreate their mortal form.

However, Philip's gift is rarer even than this form of physical mediumship. I will never forget sitting in his living room in a small suburb of East Grinstead in England, and seeing his face and body alter from that of his normal large build into a small Japanese man. Right before my eyes his features simply changed. It was not a second body of semi-physical etheric substance masking his own, it was an actual shapeshift into the form of another person. Although a Japanese man is not exactly a werewolf which is the image we commonly associate with shapeshifting and often use as a measure for the phenomenon, we need to remember that shapeshifting is all about the movement of energy and so shapeshifting can occur on any vibrational level and involve any form, be it wolfish or Japanese.

Philip had spent many years working with his Japanese spirit guide and was energetically linked to the point that a cellular shift was possible, and it is only a small conceptual bridge to cross to realise that such an energetic link may be formed with an animal guide just as readily. Furthermore, as shapeshifting is conditional upon the movement of energy, we may also entertain the notion that no particular animal spirit would even be necessary for an advanced shapeshifter. A human being could create a general energetic species link.

Few people believe however, that cellular shapeshifting really exists. Increasing numbers of people today within various new-age movements do agree that some types of shapeshifting are possible, and mental and even astral shapeshifting are thought to occur to some degree within human beings quite naturally, although most are not really aware of what is happening or are too afraid to let anyone else know that they have had a strange experience.

I discovered perhaps the most evocative and well written experience of a mental shift whilst doing some academic research into the imagination at The University of Kent. The experience was reproduced in Dr Susan Greenwood's book 'The Anthropology of Magic' and it was this account which alerted me to Richard Mabey's twilight encounter. Mabey is an Oxford educated naturalist and author and we are very fortunate that this academic felt inclined to share his experience with the public, an experience which he still regards as being extremely unusual and impossible to rationalise. In his book *A brush with nature* which is a collection of his favourite articles written by him for the BBC's *Wildlife* magazine, he tells of his twilight encounter with a nightingale:

'*The setting is narcotic. A full moon, mounds of cow parsley glowing like suspended balls of mist, the fen arching like a lustrous whaleback across the whole span of the southern horizon. The nightingale was a shaman, experienced, rhetorical, insistent. I sank into its charms, a willing initiate. A shooting star arched over the bush in which it was singing. As I edged closer, its song seemed to become solid, to be doing odd things to the light. I was aware that my peripheral vision was closing down, and that I had no sense of where I was in space. And then, for just a few seconds, the bird was in my head and it was me that was singing.*'

What a beautiful and life-changing moment this must have been. Did Mabey become the bird physically? Probably not, it seems the bird was a shaman who had already achieved the form. For Mabey it appears to have been an extremely powerful mental shift. He seems seduced and lured by the animal's spirit and there is indeed a tradition in ancient cultures of shaman turning themselves into birds and flying to others who require initiation or healing, so Mabey's instinct that the nightingale was a shaman is probably correct. The shaman may have come to him that night to impart a shapeshifting experience to awaken his latent psychic abilities and change the focus of his life.

Mabey's description of the experience entails a marked change of sensory perception. He can see the sound waves of the song becoming visible as energy whilst the vibration of light equally begins to morph. The normal constructs of space and time disintegrate as human and nightingale merge and commune in song. Interestingly, Richard Mabey has now written a book based upon a personal exploration and journey with the nightingale called *The Barley Bird*, we may assume the moonlit shamanic encounter had a profound effect upon him and his future work.

Such moments of spontaneous merging are extremely rare although these moments can, and sometimes do occur, between witches and their familiars. The romantic view of the ancient wicce concocting spells with her plump black cat overseeing the process is not just a fancy, animal helpers were considered to be vital companions who would often represent the wicce's own intuitive capabilities. A familiar is much more than just a pet, although many pet owners do have some extraordinary experiences of communication with their animal. Unlike a pet however, a familiar is not owned or possessed by the wicce or witch. The relationship is one of mutual respect and communion and no familiar would willingly work with a wicce in servitude as this would diminish their vital energy.

I have often read in modern witch lore that a familiar must be 'empowered' to become a magical helper. Unfortunately this misconception is a symptom of our modern societal belief that humanity exists within a hierarchical structure of existence with humans at the top, animals lower down and aspects of the natural world such as rocks firmly at the bottom. However, similarly to chapter two where I explained that traditionally, herbs were not 'empowered' but rather 'compelled' to reveal their already powerful, potent nature, the same is true of a familiar. The idea that we need to empower any animal would cause any wicce or shaman to shake their head in complete wonderment at our modern arrogance.

By 'compel' I do not mean of course that we must control our familiar through an act of dominant 'will' as is sometimes the high magical custom but rather, like the herbs, we compel quite naturally when we recognise and experience our similarity of spirit with our familiar and merge together in a combined nature. It is our unity of energy with the animal and natural world which compels their revealing, a recognition therefore that we are the same, not above or superior to any other being.

I have also read that one should not have a black coated familiar unless one is a very experienced shapeshifter or witch. Apparently this is because the colour black naturally attracts and benefits negative energies and malevolent entities. This is again a misconception from our confused modern and christianised society.

In many cultures the colour black is considered extremely positive in its nature, vibrating in sympathy with the ideals of wisdom, rebirth and fertility. Others still argue to the contrary that black has a lower vibration than white for example, and is therefore closer to the earth element. Even if this latter notion is the case, which I believe it is, it does not necessarily follow that this makes black 'negative' or 'more evil' than other colours. To put it bluntly, if a colour like black really does determine that we will encounter negative energies, then many indigenous shamanic cultures with beautiful ebony skins would be in deep trouble. Cutting up our world and experiences into good/bad, positive/negative, black/white dualities is an illusion made by ourselves. I have no doubt that any witch with a black cat is a very content witch indeed.

Odin, the great God of the Anglo-Saxons was equally content to have two familiars in the form his black crows called Huginn and Muninn. Each morning he would send them out into the world to report back to him with any news that may be important for the coming day. It has been speculated that the crows were representative of Odin's thoughts and memories, with one crow Huginn, being the cognitive one processing all that he encounters whilst Muninn stores all the information as memories which can be used and retrieved at a later date when required. There is thus a merging of faculties between Odin and his familiars. When his crows fly, part of Odin himself flies with them witnessing all they see.

Similar traditions are reported from shamanic tribes across the planet and those surviving today still shapeshift or 'soul merge' with birds in order to fly the skies and perceive the world from this different perspective. Indonesian shamans have used this skill for millennia to help navigate the seas. As a bird they are able to fly far out from the land and report back as to the wind-direction and weather conditions.

The contemporary author Philip Pullman has delivered an extremely accurate representation of the nature and connection of familiars to their human. Pullman's 'His Dark Materials' trilogy is set in a parallel universe which although similar to our own retains certain subtle differences which although existing in our reality, are unfortunately hidden from us.

In his beautifully constructed alternate universe people have daemon's, not evil spirits of course but rather, animal counterparts who embody the intuitive aspect or soul-self of their human. These familiars work with and advise their human in all things, at times disagreeing with their human and becoming quite upset and angry with them. The bond between human and familiar is extremely strong and within the story, when the Church, depicted as the magisterium attempts to cut human children from their familiars this results in soulless children, lost, ill and tormented. Also, if a familiar strays too far from their human then both feel actual physical as well as emotional and spiritual pain. I believe Pullman's literary depiction of the mental shifting which may occur between familiars and humans to be extremely accurate.

Actual documented accounts of the wicce's use of animal familiars surface most readily within the detailed transcripts and materials from the infamous witch trials in England and in particular those from the county of Essex. Within the early trials which began in the fifteenth century, familiars took a central role as one of the main evaluative items of evidence against an accused witch. Although most witch trials record a mind-boggling array of hysterical and obviously fanciful fabrication, the early trials which occurred before the hysteria really set in do seem to retain some semblance of sanity.

Transcripts of the early trials reveal how the witch's familiar was thought to *always works with the witch in everything*, a quotation taken from the infamous witch inquisitor's handbook of 1486. Therefore, there was a common belief that every witch would have a familiar and if the familiar could be so identified, then this could be used in evidence against them. Unfortunately this meant that as time went on, any person living alone with a pet for company was in deep danger of being tried for witchcraft.

The early trials all seem agree on certain features of behaviour between witches and their familiars, behaviours which do appear reasonable when compared with what we have learnt of the wicce so far. For example, familiars were always described as having approached the wicce rather than being sought as a pet or helper. The familiar would already have name and would only assist the wicce in equal partnership, meaning that if the familiar disagreed with the intent of the working or action, it would often refuse to help and warn instead of possible consequences.

As witch trials became more macabre however, familiars were viewed increasingly as evil demonic entities which would urge the wicce to commit terrible acts of dark malefic magic against others. During the most infamous of English witch trials, the Pendle case which occurred in Lancashire in 1612 it was recorded how a familiar, a black dog called Dandy, had approached a wicce (although by the middle ages the Old English term 'wicce' had evolved into our modern term 'witch') called James Device to conduct image magic against a local woman named as Mistris Towneley. The familiar *bade this examinate* [the accused witch] *make a picture of clay, like unto the said Mistris Towneley: and that this examinate with the helpe of his spirit (who then euer after bidde this examinate call it Dandy) would kill or destroy the said Mistris Towneley*.

Within the confessions of the Pendle witches from 1612 and later trials in Pendle in 1633, we find comments indicating that certain familiars appeared to be able to change their form into other animals, and even into human forms. This has led some later researches to speculate that perhaps the familiars were in fact the witches themselves who, having shapeshifted, met together in animal guise in order to escape being seen during this dangerous time. One of the accused, Margaret Johnson, explained that when a witch wished to travel by magic, they would assume the shape of their animal guide but not from the *'substance of their bodies, but their spirit assumeth such form and shape as go into such rooms.'* This seems to indicate a type of shapeshift akin to Odin, where the consciousness of the wicce can form a mental energetic link with the familiar and travel with them to other locations.

Mental shapeshifting abilities could also be used for darker intents however, and peculiar to Anglo-Saxon England was a powerful type of shifting spell called 'The Sending'. The spell required the wicce to create a thought form which was normally said to be that of a wolf or nightwalker, which would be sent to another person to feed from their life force and bring about their death. The Sending worked upon the ancient belief that fear leaves one open to the appetites of darkly things, and so the thought form would tap into the unfortunate recipients deepest fears, weakening their resolve over a number of days until the dark entity could suck its fill completely. The notion that fear opens us up to negativity is familiar to us today as increasing numbers of new-age spiritual paths teach a very similar principle.

Confessions of witches during the burning times have often been dismissed as unreliable, as any confession taken under torture is spurious indeed. However, one of the enduring mysteries of the Pendle case is that the witches, who were mostly all from one family who all lived together, were not forced to confess under torture. The confessions were given freely and further, the family members all accused each other of committing murders using image magic and familiars. It is obvious from the confessions that each had some knowledge of what today we would term dark magic, but it is quite possible that by this time in history, given the growing witch hysteria, that such practices were commonly known to form the central evidence within witchcraft trials. Perhaps the Pendle witches simply hated each other, perhaps the family were involved in a murder and wished to move the guilt to another and saw this as the most effective platform, perhaps they simply loved being in the limelight or perhaps, they truly were witches who had ravaged the community with their thirst for dark magic and had finally been caught. We will never know for sure why they confessed so readily to such colourful and extensive stories of dark witchcraft.

Moving back in time before the Old English term '*wiccecræft*' evolved into 'witchcraft' we begin to find many more references to shapeshifting. It seems our wicce brothers and sisters of the ancient Craft felt quite comfortable with the practice, inspired as it was by the Gods of Old. One of our most enduring representations of the ancient wicce is the figure of the witch seated upon her broomstick, with a black cat seated behind silhouetted against the light of the full moon. This popular and nowadays cartoon image of the witch is often considered to be little more than romanticised fiction of a burning times emblem, which was designed to strike fear into the souls of good Christian folk.

However, when we look back to the Anglo-Saxon and Nordic documents such as the *Prose Edda,* written by Snorri Sturluson in or around 1220 although depicting events generally considered to be rather earlier, we find a world filled with such enigmatic images. Within the *Prose Edda* Sturluson describes the Earth Goddess Freya as being one of the last great Goddesses of Northern Europe to survive the relentless forces of the new Christian God. Freya was commonly depicted as flying high upon her staff or broomstick across the night sky with her familiar, a black cat, flying behind her. The Goddess was renowned for her shapeshifting abilities and her preferred animal form was feline, specifically, a big black cat. Her shifting would be induced after extensive preparations including fasting, chanting and incantations.

Perhaps the most famous shapeshifter of Anglo-Saxon England however, was the great Odin himself. We have already found him to be a powerful mental shifter, flying the lands with his two black crows but Odin was also known to shapeshift physically too and the form he most commonly adopted was that of the eagle. Odin also required preparations to achieve his cellular shifting, but for him a psychotropic concoction served better than incantations and chanting. Odin would drink '*The mead which forth from Surtr's sunk dales the Strong-through-spells swift-flying bore,*' and after his drinking was seen to change into a great eagle whilst holding some of the concoction in his beak to bring to others who had abilities to 'compose' themselves into other forms. It is further told that Odin's wolves were not necessarily animal familiars but were actually skilled wicce who acted as sacred priestesses for Odin. These powerful wicce were able to shapeshift into different animal forms overseen by the Goddess Freya, and were known commonly as the *wælcyrge* the warrior maidens responsible for bringing the spirits of the battle dead safely into Valhalla.

In the lacnunga we are told how the *wælcyrge* would ride out over the battle field to claim the spirits of the dead and dying, and how their claim could be thwarted for the lucky few who knew such magic:

'*Hlude wæron hy la hlude ða hy ofer þone hlæw ridan wæran anmode ða hy ofer land ridan. Scyld ðu ðe nu þu ðysne genesan mote. Ut lytel spere gif her inne sie. Stod under linde under leohtum scylde þær ða mihtigan wif hyra mægen beræddon ond hy gyllende garas sændan ic him oðerne eft wille sændan, fleogende flanae forane togeanes.'*

'Loud were they, Lo! Loud as they rode over the barrow, they were determined as they rode over the land. Shield yourself now, so you may escape this attack. Out, little spear, if it be in here. I stood under linden, under a light shield, where the mighty women declared their might and yelling they sent spears. Back to them I wish to send another, a flying dart in opposition.'

Physical shifting enjoys a long and rich heritage within Europe and particularly England. Our shamanic sisters and brothers of the Craft were able to transform themselves at will although it is likely that some were more specialised in this ability than others. However, the dominant and enduring image we have of the shapeshifting phenomenon comes to us as the werewolf, and no writer on this subject can do it justice without delving into this mysterious wolfish world.

It is unsurprising that Clarrisa Pinkola Estés' book 'Women who run with the Wolves', remained on the *New York Times* best seller list for 145 weeks, just the title of the work captivates and enchants us before we have read a single word. Although Estés approaches the familial relationship between women and wolves within a psychological paradigm, the stories she uses are evocative, and the insights in her prose awaken a remembering within our spirit. After reading her book I cannot believe that I am the only woman in the world to have found a quiet spot of woodland and howled with the full moon!

Hollywood has brought werewolves right into our living rooms, prowling and growling when we watch block buster films such as the Twilight trilogy. When the film is over we return to the mundane often thinking our movie encounter to be pure escapist fiction, far removed from the real world of job, house-work and compromise. How many of us continue unconsciously to feel our paws padding across the floor as our etheric body remembers how good it feels to run free and wild? How easy would it be to give in to the impulse and simply allow the fur to come and the snout, the ears and tail? Is the movie depiction so far from a potential reality? I will state this unequivocally, the answer is no. Liberties with the truth are obviously taken, sometimes with abundance but the kernel remains as a consistent reminder that what we see upon our TV and cinema screens is the product of millennia of experience.

The werewolf legacy in these British Iles has been traced by researchers and academics back to Odin's soldiers called the *Úlfheðnar,* or the Beserkers as they are more commonly known to us today. The word beserker is thought to derive from one of two possible origins, firstly *baresark* meaning a man who is 'bare of shirt' or *bearsark,* meaning one who wears the pelt of the bear as a shirt. The *Úlfheðnar* however, wore wolf skins more than bear skins so it seems probable that the former word may be etymologically correct despite the current contestations. Our English phrase 'going berserk' has reached through the centuries from these fearsome warriors to the modern day describing a person who appears to have completely lost control to a fit of frenzied rage, where normal rational thinking and reason disintegrate into a chaos of primal, deep seated emotion and fury.

Today we are educated by the current psychotherapeutic tradition into thinking that hatred, rage and anger are negative emotions emerging from deep fears usually stemming from childhood traumas, neglect, feelings of being unwanted, unloved and fear of our own mortality. The *Úlfheðnar* however, could not be described as fearful in the slightest, in fact, completely the opposite, they welcomed an honourable death although if legend and surviving documents are to be believed, death rarely came to them.

The *Úlfheðnar* were not just warriors or soldiers, they were initiates into a specific cult of Odin who practiced many magical rites focused upon shapeshifting which was induced through the supping of Odin's herbal psychotropic mead combined with Freya's dancing, chanting and invocations. There are ornaments surviving from Anglo-Saxon times depicting such dancing with warriors wearing wolf and bear skins. There are also the accounts from Sturluson, and epic literature such as Beowulf lending their mythic authority to these ancient ceremonies.

Once a state of frenzy had been induced the warriors were battle ready, armed with little more than their wolf skins, swords and axes. Despite such little armoury or protection, witnesses said that *'no weapon could bite them'* and *'blades and weapons glanced off them'* as if the *Úlfhéðnar* were possessed of an Otherworldly magic enveloping them with a spell of immortality. In *Havamál*, Óðinn tells of the spells he uses to secure this immunity, and as is often the case in ancient magic, spells are sung:

> *A third song I know, if sore need should come*
> *of a spell to stay my foes;*
> *When I sing that song, which shall blunt their swords,*
> *nor their weapons nor staves can wound.*

It is further said that the physical appearance of the *Úlfhéðnar* was far from normal, with their great wolf pelts and distorted features which some described as giving the affect of ugly trolls who would emit unearthly howlings, screechings and biting of their own shields. In *Egil's Saga* Egil is himself described as being extremely ugly with matted black hair, a terrible stare and eyebrows which meet in the middle! The terrible frenzy which accompanied this grotesque and terrifying sight leading to success on the battle field, had the unfortunate effect of being so consuming and powerful that the spells continued to work long after the battle was won, creeping into everyday life. As the researcher Howard Fabing describes:

> *'This fury, which was called berserkergang, occurred not only in*

the heat of battle, but also during laborious work. Men who were thus seized performed things which otherwise seemed impossible for human power. This condition is said to have begun with shivering, chattering of the teeth, and chill in the body, and then the face swelled and changed its colour. With this was connected a great hot-headedness, which at last gave over into a great rage, under which they howled as wild animals, bit the edge of their shields, and cut down everything they met without discriminating between friend or foe. When this condition ceased, a great dulling of the mind and feebleness followed, which could last for one or several days.'

(*'On going beserk, A Neurochemical Inquiry'*, 1956)

An experienced *Úlfhéðnar* therefore, no longer required ritualistic or psychotropic induction to shapeshift, as the change would continue to occur quite naturally and often spontaneously. In *Egils' Saga* we are told of *Ulf*, a retired *Úlfhéðnar* who was still overcome by the frenzy or beserkergang years after his active service in Odin's army had ceased. When evening came Ulf would become uncommunicative and ill-tempered, taking early to his bed. People called him *Kveld-Ulf* which meant 'evening wolf', as he was thought to be a shapeshifter disappearing after dark into the dense forest only to return to his bed the following morning, tired and muddy.

Belief in werewolves has persisted into our present day with a wealth of different myths and laws surrounding them such as their need for a full moon, and their unfortunate allergy to silver. However, even these apparently fictitious traditions find a lengthy and ancient heritage beyond their Hollywood depictions. The full moon has been known as a time of heightened natural energy probably since the beginning of our time. Today, science has proven that natural electrical energies which occur within our world are indeed effected by the lunar cycle and therefore, people who find their moods changing when a full moon approaches are not 'loony' in a bad way, in fact, a lunar reaction is quite normal and if recognised, can be used for many magical works especially healing and of course, other transformations too.

As for an allergy to silver, we may assume that a silver bullet would indeed kill a werewolf but as many have argued, wouldn't any type of bullet or weapon work just as well, isn't the whole 'silver thing' just evidence of the nonsense and fiction surrounding werewolves? Perhaps, but silver has always held a sacred position in magical practices with its energies allied to the moon and the dark of night, which is a time when the boundaries between this and the Otherworld are most permeable. To shapeshift requires a strong Otherworldly connection and it was thought that silver would thus cause damage to the werewolf not just within this world but also, if the werewolf should try to escape into the Otherworld, the silver would have greater effect there too. Therefore, our modern depictions retain this ancient knowledge, despite the understanding being long forgotten.

A further popular werewolf law states that if a person is bitten by a werewolf, then they will become a werewolf too. This belief combines the memories of the *Úlfhéðnar* with healing knowledge which increasingly viewed frenzy and irrational behaviour as an illness or contagion. It was thought that a malevolent entity from the Otherworld was to blame for the werewolf phenomenon and therefore ordinary men and women if bitten, would fall prey to infection and begin exhibiting symptoms of wolfish transformation. So terrified were the people of dark ages England of such infection, there are surviving accounts in Bald's Leechbook of three remedies which were known to be given to victims of werewolf bites:

1- Wiþ deofolseoce do on halig wæter ond on eala bisceopwyrte, hindhioloþan, agrimonian, Alexandrian, gyþrifan, sele him drincan. Eft, cassuc, þefan þorn, stancrop, elehtre, finul, eoforprote, cropleac, ofgeot gelice. Eft spiwedrenc wið deofle, nim micle hand fulle secges ond glædenan, do on þannan, geot micelne bollan fulne ealaþ on, bewyl healf, gegnid xx lybcorna, do on þæt, þis is god drenc wiþ deofle.

'For devilsickness, put into holy water and into ale bishopwort, hindhealth, agrimony, Alexandria, cockle, give it to him to drink. Again, hassock, hawthorn, stonecrop, lupin, fennel, boarthroat, cropleek, pour out likewise. Again, a powerful drink for a devil: take a large handful of sedge, and of gladdon, put it into a pan, pour a large bowlful of ale over it, boil away to half, crush twenty libcorns, add them to it. This is a good drink for a devil.'

2- Wiþ þon þe mon sie monaþseoc, nim mereswines fel, wyrc to swipan, swing mid þone man, sona bið sel, amen.

For that one be moon-mad, take a dolphin's hide, make it into a scourge, beat the person, he will soon be better.

3- Leoht drenc wiþ wedenheorte, elehtre, bisceopwyrt, ælfþone, elene, cropleac, hindhiolope, ontre, clate, nim þas wyrta þonne dæg ond niht scade, sing ærest on ciricean letania ond credan ond pater noster. Gang mid þy sange to þam wyrtum, ymbga hie þriwa ær þu hie nime ond ga eft to ciricean, gesing xii mæssan ofer þam wyrtum þonne þu hie ofgoten hæbbe.

A light drink for a frenzy: lupin, bishopswort, elfthon, elecampane, cropleek, hindhealth, radish, burdock; take these plants when day and night divide, sing the litany first in church, and the 'credo', and 'pater noster', go while singing to the plants, go round them thrice, before you take them and go back to the church and sing twelve masses over the plants when you have steeped them.

The third remedy is one of those peculiar half heathen half Christian healing rituals where the credo and the mass usurped the original pagan chants and adorations. Also within Bard's Leechbook, is a charm to be used against the evil doings of various spirits or beings including elves and shadow-walkers. Shadow-walkers were peculiar to the forests of England and were thought to be shapeshifters who had the ability to walk between the worlds. Their Old English name was *sceadugenga* or *nihtgengan* (nightwalkers), which some have linked to an ancient English Vampire tradition:

Wyrc sealfe wiþ ælfcynne ond nihtgengan ond þam mannum þe deofol mid hæmð, genim eowohumelan, wermod, bisceopwyrt, elehtre, æscþtoe, beolone, harewyrt, haransprecel, hæþbergean wisan, cropleac, garleac, hegerifan corn, gyþrife, finul; do þas wyrta on an fæt, sete under weofod, sing ofer viiii mæssan awyl on buteran ond on sceapes smerwe, do haliges sealtes fela on, aseoh þurh clað, weorp þa wyrta on yrnende wæter. Gif men hwilc yfel costing weorþe oþþe ælf oþþe nihtgengan, smire his ond wlitan mid þisse sealfe ond on his Eagan do, ond þær him se lichoma sar sie, ond recelsa hine ond sena gelome, his þing biþ sona selre.

Make a salve for the elvish race, and nightgoers, and the people with whom the devil has intercourse, take ewehumble, wormwood, bishopswort, lupin, ashthroat, henbane, harewort, whortleberry shoots, cropleek, garlic, hedgerive, corn cockle, fennel, put these plants into a vessel, set it under an alter, sing nine masses over it, boil in butter and in sheep's grease, add a lot of holy salt, strain through a cloth, throw the plants into running water. If any evil temptation should befall one, or an elf, or a nightgoer, let him smear his face with this salve, and put it on his eyes, and where his body may be sore, and smoke him, and make the sign over him often, his case will soon be better.

The view that shapeshifting into a werewolf was caused by a malevolent infectious spirit, had the unfortunate implication that this particular form of shift was believed to be beyond the control of the victim. To be gripped by such a frenzy without any hope of personal control over one's symptoms would have been a terrifying experience. However, as Joseph Campbell has argued, the closest we seem to come in our modern world to such a situation is within the labels of schizophrenic or psychotic mental illness, and if only we could embrace the shamanic understanding of our magical consciousness then perhaps some of today's schizophrenics could be guided in learning to control and even welcome their unique view of the world, and become our modern shamans, healers, witches and teachers instead of carrying the stigma of abnormality.

Let us now move further back through time, to before the dark ages, and discover even older seeds of shapeshifting lore. In the time before Christianity recast supernatural experiences which occurred outside of the Church as evil, irrational and beyond human control an entirely different picture of shifting emerges.

Fifteen thousand years ago in southern France, shapeshifting was a necessary and normal part of tribal community life. Deep within the caverns of Les Trois Fréres so named after the three brothers who discovered them in 1910, is a remarkable series of pre-historic cave paintings. It is extremely difficult to get to the paintings physically as they are to be found along deep, long and very narrow tunnels which will suddenly open into vast cavernous cathedrals before returning again to their narrow journey into the earth. Just getting there must have been an extraordinary experience for ancient peoples with no electric torches and hard hats.

The most famous image which has made these particular caves so well known is the figure of the 'dancing shaman' or sorcerer. It is commonly held that the image has the legs of a human being, the paws of a bear, the tail of a horse, the eyes of an owl, the ears of a wolf and the antlers of a deer. It has further been suggested that the unusual block shading used by this pre-historic artist, may represent the internal skeletal and muscular structures of the body. If so, then perhaps the artist is indeed indicating that a physical transformation is occurring here.

The shaman presides over a magnificent scene of bison running, and within the herd of bison is a further shaman who appears to be playing a drum. The way the paintings are positioned within the cavern suggests a ceremonial alter, and anthropologists agree that there is evidence of ritualistic activity within the space.

Hunting would have been a principle focus and activity of the ancient tribe which existed around Les Trois Fréres, and it is commonly accepted that the images were inspired by this necessity for food and were used to encourage the old gods to ensure a successful hunt. The figure of the shaman certainly presides above the apparent wild hunt although it is interesting to note that no bison are being killed in the picture but rather, the shaman are running or journeying with the bison like kindred spirits.

Gerald Gardner also mentions the caves of Les Trois Fréres and the dancing shaman, in his meticulously researched book 'The Meaning of Witchcraft'. He was fascinated by these early depictions of magical works and identified the small figurines of animals pierced with spears which have sometimes been found in these caves, to be evidence of the development of magic as a sympathetic dialogue between reality and desired intention. He did not make the further jump to consider the possibility of shapeshifting, yet this is not surprising given that anthropologists had yet to bring the phenomenon to the attention of the wider academic audience. (Gardner also discovered an ancient depiction within another cave formation of women circling a man with one woman wielding a ritualistic knife!)

What these cave paintings appear to demonstrate is that ancient shamanic cultures, as well as those surviving into Christianised modernity such as the wicce, honoured the animal spirits which fed and nourished them. They lived side by side animals in a relationship of mutual respect and reciprocity, honouring them and journeying with their spirits into the Otherworld.

In almost all surviving cave paintings we see similar scenes of beautifully crafted and surprisingly sophisticated animal paintings, employing artistic skills of perspective and movement. In marked contrast however, are the human figures which occur. Most are extremely crude appearing more like stick men alongside the majestic bison and horse. I do not believe that this is due to our ancestor's inability to draw humans; they would have possessed the same keen observation for the human form as they would have the animal form. From the research I have done into shamanic cultures, it seems more likely that this stark contrast occurs because the shaman losses his commitment to the human form when he journeys with the animal spirits during shapeshifting.

It is true that the dancing sorcerer of Les Trois Fréres appears to be a rather confused shapeshifter, attempting to change into a variety of animals at the same time. Many modern writers assert that this is simply not possible and the ancient figure is thus a metaphorical ritualistic image, which does not depict actual shapshifting ability. However, reports of multiple shifting are not so uncommon. In sixteenth century England a young woman called Agnus Brown was walking home when she saw *'a thynge lyke a black dogge with a face like an ape, a short taile, a cheine and a syluer whystle about its neck, and a peyre of hornes on his heade.'* Agnus was not the only one to have seen this creature, which was commonly believed to be linked to a local wicce in some way. Shamans have the ability to change into many forms although it is certainly extremely difficult to merge into many in the same moment. So let us now move on to discuss the 'how' of shapeshifting abilities more fully.

How to shapeshift mentally

The first thing to remember is that everything is energy. The book you are holding in your hands, the thoughts occurring within your mind and the feelings which you are currently experiencing are all energy, vibrating at differing frequencies.

This is because we and everything that exists from the physical to the non-physical was created from the same source, the explosion of high density energy. Every star, planet, microbe, plant, bacteria and object is thus formed of the same star dust which is always in flux. Nothing is static. This means that on an essential primordial level, everything is connected.

Physicists have discovered in recent decades that the particles which serve as the building blocks of matter are in fact, like little pods of vibrational energy and are not therefore, actually physical. Oddly, as scientists within the strange and mysterious field of quantum mechanics have realised, particles only appear to become static and thus physical, when they are observed.

If we can embrace the understanding that essentially, we are composed of the same energy as the animals, stars and plants then the boundaries which force us to live within our limited world view begin to move. Possibilities that we had never considered real, from telepathy to shapeshifting and more, suddenly become tantalisingly familiar. The most important step towards shapeshifting is to believe that what has always seemed impossible is in fact, possible. What we believe in, we give energy to and this constructs our experience. If at heart you believe you will never shapeshift or that really, shapeshifting just isn't possible then you won't shift, it's that simple. You cannot move energy that you don't believe is there, and shapeshifting is all about the movement of energy.

A good way to begin is by trying some mental shifting. To do this you will need a pet or familiar, although if you don't have an animal at home then take a walk to a local park where there will be many birds singing in the trees who will help you just as readily. When you have an animal in view then take some deep centring breathes and relax deeply. Let any distractions drift away. Any thoughts, any concerns which haunt you can just drift through your mind without you needing to hold onto or comment on them. When you feel that you are in a comfortable light trance state, then imagine what it is like to see the world from your animal's point of view. What can they see? Then imagine you are the animal. How do they feel? Allow your imagination to take you further and truly inhabit the body and mind of your animal. Stretch into the four legs or into the wings, feel the wind blowing your fur or feather or whatever feels appropriate for your context. Move with your animal when they move. Try not to analyse what is happening or worry too much about becoming your animal. You cannot 'be' if you are 'becoming'. Regular practice of this exercise will lead to the type of shift experienced by Odin with his Crows, where your consciousness merges and travels with the animal you have chosen.

An alternative version of the above is to mentally shift with an animal guide. If you do not have an animal guide then you can welcome one to you by engaging your alchemical imagination. Relax as normal, in the ways already detailed, and when you feel you are in a light trance state then allow your imagination to take you to a beautiful place. Perhaps you will go to woodland, a mountain or somewhere familiar where you always felt close to nature. When you are there you may ask for your animal spirit guide to join you. As ever, just allow things to unfold without too much direction. Don't force a particular animal form.

Often, the animal we think we are closest too and which should be our animal guide, is completely the wrong animal. You may feel like a 'cat person' but discover your guide is a white horse whilst your preferred shapeshifting species is mainly canine. Do not fret; as you open to the experience of shapeshifting then these apparent contradictions begin to make sense. Different types of shifting require at times, different animal energies. For example, animal guides or personal totems as they are also called, often take on a particular role as guide and protector. A recent depiction of such a guide has entered our homes within the Harry Potter films and books, although I wonder how many realise that the 'patronus charm' (animal patron charm) actually works?

To wander into the Potteresque for a brief moment, the patronus charm is surprisingly interesting and worthy of a mention here as it is a form of shapeshifting which has now entered the homes and psyches of millions of people, including our youngest minds thanks to J.K.Rowling. The charm is an extension of mental shifting which includes a strong emotional element and a movement of the etheric body, which morphs into the shape of our totem animal. What is particularly interesting about J.K.Rowling's account is the importance she gives to the focus, intention and confidence (or belief) of the mental and emotional attitude required to achieve the shift. Furthermore, the totem animal is to be brought forward at times of great danger as a protection from evil and negativity, as it is the animal persona which is able to overcome the danger rather than the human, and this chimes with shapeshifting lore.

As our animal selves, we evaluate and experience our world quite differently from our human selves. As our animal we are unbounded by social norms, the expectations of others and our past regrets and fears. All our conditioning falls away in animal form which enables us to move beyond human categories and respond to situations in entirely different and perhaps more appropriate ways. If we project our totem animal self into a difficult situation it can overwhelm and diffuse the event entirely, where our human self, weighed down by social and personal baggage may have made matters far worse.

Physical shifting

Moving rapidly on, let us now consider taking this work to the next level, the physical shift. For this work you need to become aware of which animal or species you feel most drawn to for physical shifting. It may be the same animal you have already worked with for your mental shifting, or it could be completely different. Some wicce find that their family have a totem animal, a tribal guide which is linked to the energy of all members, and legends abound with stories of whole families of werewolves or great cats. The Isle of Lewis in Scotland was apparently home to a large family of shapeshfifters whose totem was the wolf.

I had always thought myself to be a large cat, a leopard perhaps but could not shake the desire to howl like a wolf and whenever I actually imagined physically being an animal, it was always wolfish. So spend some time experimenting with what it would be like to physically be a cat, wolf, fox, bird etc until you feel more in tune with one animal than you do the others. Many people stay committed to their chosen animal for life, although as the images of shamanic shifting indicate; this is not fixed in stone. When you have an animal in mind then play a little. Imagine being the animal, perhaps even act like the animal when no one is around. Adopt their behaviour, observe them whenever possible and learn as much as you can about them.

To physically shift requires much energy and when you feel ready to make a start, having played and learnt as much as you can until you truly feel connected to your animal, as if perhaps you really could be one yourself given the right circumstances, then progress on to the next ritual.

Ritual for physical shapeshifting

You will be creating a sacred space dedicated to the animal you feel yourself to be. Wearing loose clothes, collect any things which feel close to your animal. If you are a wolf then you may like to have some wolfish pictures for example, or even some raw steak for food. If you are outside you may like to construct a den with a bed of ferns and leaves. When your space is prepared then cast a circle in the way described in chapter three. Next, using a drum or something which makes a deep drumming sound, begin beating a rhythm, whatever rhythm feels right to you. As you beat, feel the energy in your body increasing from the base of your spine, up through the body to the top of your head. Feel the energy surrounding you like a second skin, which is a little more fluid than your physical body but dense enough to be visible. When you feel energised then hold the image of your animal in mind and remember how it feels to be that animal from the playing you have done.

Put all of your focus and intention into being your animal. Experience the feelings from your playing, the covering of fur or feather, the point of view and the behaviours. Drum for as long as feels necessary and stop when and if you wish. If all ingredients come together, the heightened energy, the focus, belief, confidence and intent then shapeshifting may occur. Do not be disappointed however, if no physical transformation happens for some time. Cellular movement is so alien to our culture it can take much effort before the disbelief drains away sufficiently for such an experience to begin. You may continue to experience mental shifts and perhaps progress through a series of etheric transformations before any physical changes occur at all. Just have patience and enjoy the journey.

After the ritual, if there is an abundance of energy remaining within you then visualise roots coming out from the bottom of your feet and burying themselves deep in the earth. Let the excess energy drain away back to the earth where it will energise and heal our great Mother. Eat and drink something to make sure you are fully grounded before dismantling the circle as before. Repeat this small ritual often and your experience will deepen and intensify every time.

If you believe that you will shift and have no fear of doing so, then the above ritual will have results. You may shift physically or the etheric body, your second skin may assume the shape of your animal as a partial cellular shift. Many books carry warnings about shapeshifting and it is worth considering these now. Shifting is indeed a powerful experience although it is unlikely anything will happen unless you are actually ready for it. Nonetheless, it is certainly a good idea to begin within the circle with your spirit guides helping you, it doesn't matter if you don't know your spirit guides, simply ask them to help and they will be with you. The only real 'danger' that is commonly described is that when you become your animal it is so liberating, you may not wish to return.

In reality, if a shift occurs then whenever you begin thinking as a human again, giving thought to whether you would like to return, then you will snap back rather quickly! If you have sufficient skill that the human thinking mind does not dominate, then you are proficient enough to return at will anyway. If you choose not to return then it will be a choice within your control. If you are unsure, then ask your spirit guides to always protect you and guide you back when they feel it is necessary.

Shapeshifting is a magical process. It involves above all, a movement of energy and a change of perception in order to achieve the desired result. The wicce saw energy as a magical elixir which permeated the worlds and every movement, every change no matter how small was viewed as a magical occurrence. Before moving on to chapter five which focuses on the full rituals and magic of the shamanic wicce in a modern context, it is necessary to make a short exploration of two conflicting definitions of what constitutes magic.

Magic and its definitions

For our ancestors and their wicce advisors, magic imbued the world. From the mundane rituals of daily life to the great feast days of celebration, magic was tangible and real. As the middle ages historian Richard Kieckhefer explains, the great sagas which have immortalised the lives of our ancestors *'depict magic as occurring amid realistic accounts of everyday situations: in the thick of family feuds, in the exercise of judicial business, in the ordinary grind of life, not in a fantasy world or an idealized or enchanted realm.'*

Every action and thought from the smallest to the greatest therefore, was an act of magic. Although many modern witches try to re-capture this wonderment of daily reality, there is an implicit assumption at work within modern magical traditions which contradicts the wicce experience. If we are to re-enchant our world and regain a living and meaningful experience of witchcraft and life in general, we must fully understand the nature of this deep and mostly unconscious contradiction which is confusing the heart of contemporary witchcraft.

The common modern definition of magic adhered to in some form by almost all followers of high magic and many modern witches today, is *'the science and art of causing change to occur in conformity with will.'* This was actually the definition popularised by the magician and Golden Dawn member Aleister Crowley. Crowley appears quite clear however, that the 'will' he referred to was the personal will of the magician and not the divine or universal 'will' which pervades the natural world, although I do acknowledge there is much controversy on this point. Nonetheless, there is an implicit energetic assumption within our modern magic working that the will of the magician is paramount, and it is this belief which now requires some further explanation if we are to fully embrace the ancient Craft of the wicce.

Crowley's maxim which supports his definition of magical practice is *'Do what thou wilt is the whole of the law, love is the law, love under will.'* This motto which forms the central philosophy of the Crowleyan 'magickal' perspective, differentiates Love from Will. Love is indeed recognised as the law of divine essence which forms the foundation of the creative life force of the universe, however, the maxim explicitly places this divine essence under and thus subordinate to, human 'will'.

It has been suggested that perhaps what Crowley really meant, was that the 'will' actually refers to the human will in unity with the divine and therefore, as Love is the Law, and to do your will is the whole of the Law, then human and divine will are thus combined. Unfortunately, this does not take care of the remaining caveat *'love under will.'* Some are now choosing to change this caveat to read *'love in unity with will'* which I feel is preferable.

Crowley was in fact, simply continuing an already embedded assumption which was seeded thousands of years earlier with the words:

'Let us make man in our image, after our likeness. They will have dominion over the fish of the sea and the birds of the heavens and over the livestock and over all the earth and over every creeping thing that creeps on the earth.'

(Genesis 1:26)

This short passage which we have ingested and regurgitated in many forms for millennia, is perhaps the first evidence of mankind's real 'fall' from grace and wisdom. It marks the point where humanity began to perceive itself as superior to the natural world and when this occurred, our separation and isolation from Mother Earth, and the interconnected experience of the creative magical universe was born. We became dominators, our aspiration became power and our tool of choice became the ego.

The results of this assumption of human domination and hierarchy needs little description or elaboration here. We see its carnage of violence, suicide, consumerism, over-population and unsustainable life styles all around us and of course, we still have the arrogance to actually force our spiritual illness onto the few shamanic cultures which have survived our attempts of destruction or assimilation. If we are ever in any doubt that our modern western world is founded on this unhealthy assumption, we just need to take a look at how we have engaged with these ancient communities and peoples.

There was once an Eden which existed and the Eden was called Mother Earth, and there is documented evidence of small pockets of this paradise which persisted right up to their 'discovery' by western cultures. In 1492 Christopher Columbus discovered the small island of Hispaniola. Detailed accounts of the voyages were kept and it was noted how the natives were friendly, generous and lived an idyllic life. The island was rich with food and forest, and the Taino tribe enjoyed a plentiful and happy existence. They had all they needed, and when the daily chores were done, they had much leisure time in which they were able to enjoy storytelling, ritual and community relationships. There is a similar story throughout the world.

The ancient tribes lived sustainably and richly, they did not suffer as we have often been led to believe. We have been given the false image of starving dirty natives living in backward societies where in fact, archaeological as well as documented observational evidence paints a very different picture. They were well fed, strong, healthy, peaceful, content. Tribes that lived in less hospitable parts of the world such as deserts and the frozen north would travel with their food sources when necessary, leading nomadic lives. There were disagreements between tribes of course but any killing was a last resort, not a route of choice. The daily work load was on average about four hours.

Today, with the increased productivity required to sustain our wholly unsustainable population, our daily work hours have soared. In many cases workers in our civilised world are struggling with such long hours that they are sleep deprived, malnourished, stressed, depressed and alone. Even the great professions to which so many have aspired such as doctors, lawyers and teachers produce conditions so appalling, that many in these professions burn out, break down and commit suicide. This is the civilised, sophisticated life style of the western world which we impose on everybody else, whether they want it or not. We do this because we think ourselves superior to Mother Earth, and those who understand and live in harmony with her. And because we are superior, we should have anything and everything we want, and what we want is more!

We must have a big house, we must have a car for each family member, we must have a number of holidays abroad, we must have all the 'things' which everybody else thinks they must have, and then we will be happy. Until then we are so scared that we don't yet have enough to be happy and secure that we become depressed, anxious, run down, stressed and despairing as our house gets bigger, our mortgage gets bigger, our car gets bigger, our credit gets bigger, our taxes get bigger, our ego gets bigger and the foundations upon which it all rests become weaker and meaningless. Crowley, despite what many think of him was a very intelligent man. He understood this dynamic, at least on some level. This was his ironic legacy disguised in his mantra; this is his *'love under will'*.

The Taino tribe were happy. They had enough. Columbus however, did not believe he had enough and wrote in 1493 of the natives of Hisapniola:

'It is possible, with the name of the holy trinity, to sell all the slaves which it is possible to sell....Here there are so many of these slaves, and also brazilwood, that although they are living things they are as good as gold.'

Thousands of the Taino were sold as slaves with those remaining on the island forced to work for the occupiers. Columbus justified his abuse of these *'living things'* as a commodity akin to gold by way of the holy trinity. The labour was hard and the hours long, for women as well as men. The younger women and girls were forced to a life of sexual slavery with repeated, abusive rape and violence. These noble and beautifully content people who welcomed Columbus became so soul destroyed, that as Pedro de Cordoba wrote to the Spanish King in 1517:

'As a result of the sufferings and hard labour they endured, the Indians (Taino) choose and have chosen suicide. Occasionally a hundred have committed mass suicide. The women, exhausted by labour, have shunned conception and childbirth... Many, when pregnant, have taken something to abort and have aborted. Others after delivery have killed their children with their own hands, so as not to leave them in such oppressive slavery.'

Although we do not engage in such overt abominations today, the impulse which drove Columbus to such horrific acts still exists in abundance, it has simply become more implicit, better justified and whenever possible, hidden.

This assumption of human supremacy stands in stark contrast to the ancient view of the wicce and our shamanic ancestors in England, Europe and the wider world. For those interested in an extremely thorough account of the full impact of the dominator mentality upon our modern world, I would highly recommend Thom Hartmann's book 'The last hours of ancient sunlight' which is a thought provoking journey to say the least, and to which I am indebted.

In contrast to the Crowleyan and arguably religious view of magic, consider now the definition by Robbyne LaPlant-Seaman which really captures the essence of the old ways of magical experience:

'Magic is finding your connection to the Earth and all that is natural, alive and moving in the universe! It binds all that exists together. Magic is living in balance with the flow of life, and knowing that you are a vital force within that flow. Magic is everywhere! In the trees, rain, stars, and in the sea. It is the spark that quickens a seed to rise up from the soil. Magic is laughter, joy, wonder and truth of the world around us! It is the subtle enchantment that reminds us not to waste a single moment of this gift that we call life! Magic is not greed, or power, or pretence...It is real. It exists. And it works. Magic is the mystery that lies in the secret soul of the world. It is the

essence of creation. What we imagine, we have the power to create!
MAGIC IS WITHIN YOU... With it you can create your dreams,
heal your world, love your life and find the peace that lives in every
human heart.'

Magic is the energy which permeates everything and everywhere.
It is a language and experience common to all the realms, flowing
with our alchemical imagination, linking, weaving and becoming
each moment. The wicce would swim these magical waters into
the Otherworld and back again, back and forth, with the breath
of our Mother as she breathes her nurturing life force to all her
children. We flow with her but we have forgotten our breath.

Very slowly, over millennia we have become increasingly
dulled and numbed, and our breathing has become shallow
and laboured. Even indigenous communities who had lived in
paradise for thousands of years were susceptible to this illness
of spirit and sight. The Maya for example, became confused,
mistaking the life force of the Mother for actual blood rather
than love. When pain and death became their central religion
and their society became so large that food became scarce, then
fear reigned as the dominator spirit took control. There are even
documented instances of wicce who resorted to cursing and harm
due to this same corroding fear sweeping our minds, crushing
our spirits. 'Will' took over whilst love receded, and fear reigned
in every heart.

Religious versus scientific magic

Our indigenous shamanic witchcraft is scientific in its
foundational concept of the world. This may appear a rather
strange statement to make considering that science today seems
so removed from magic and spiritual concerns. Science is mostly
empirical, meaning that it seeks to understand the universe through
observational data. Observation relies upon our perception and
in the dark ages, perception included the magical. What was once

included as observational data and therefore, as science, was far more inclusive of what we term the super-natural today. Modern science eschews the Otherworld because our perceptions have changed. It is most probable however, that at some point in the future, we may well be able to scientifically measure or observe the energy which we refer to as magic, as a natural part of the universe. We only call magic and its manifestations super-natural, because science cannot yet understand.

The experience that everything is interconnected and equal is natural, yet it conflicts with every foundational concept of the dominator religions. The magical traditions which have adopted the religious hierarchical dominator style cannot also work coherently with the natural scientific shamanic style of magic, yet this is exactly what many try to do.

The difference between the scientific and religious magical impulse is embedded and subtle, yet can be put simply as the difference between becoming the energy of the natural world and flowing with it to effect the changes required or alternatively, imposing desired change by commanding spirits and energy to do our will regardless of the flowing energy of the natural world. I am so pleased to say that there is indeed a growing desire in contemporary witchcraft to leave behind its religious, Crowleyan lineage and move towards a shamanic heritage, but more needs to change first if we are to re-align with the traditional Craft. Craft must come before religion. The Craft is shamanic and endures throughout time whereas religions morph and crumble, with the transitory whims of one species.

Those readers familiar with Gerald Gardner's 'The Meaning of Witchcraft' may remember his unequivocal statement that '*It must be understood clearly that witchcraft is a religion*'. Although Gardner was most certainly a formidable mind whose research into the origins of witchcraft was painstaking and thorough, he was also an anthropologist and was therefore susceptible to the prevalent research assumptions of the time. Gardner comments in his book that it is most probable that the Craft was not always allied to religious tradition. I believe Gardner was quite right with his instinct here and had he lived today, within anthropology's new contextualised assumption which no longer supposes all ritualistic practices to be necessarily evidence of religious foundation, I feel Gardner would have embraced a rather more non-religious shamanistic quality in his own Craft working.

I would suggest that if the great Gerald Gardner were here today, still researching with vigour he may revise his view regarding the religious element of Wicca and perhaps state not that witchcraft is itself a religion but rather, that witchcraft has been intimately involved with religious practices to the point of apparent interdependence for many centuries if not millennia, and this interdependence continues today.

It still appears quite natural for us to equate ritual with religion and I am not suggesting that this is necessarily wrong but rather, we need to become aware that this is an assumption not a reality. As the Otherworld became increasingly removed from our everyday world, our Gods and our very life force fragmented into this lost realm as it was ripped away from us. This fragmentation enabled the dominator religions to fill the resultant gap, (although many would argue they created it).

The gap between this world and the Otherworld then needed to be mediated, and at first there was a flexibility of mediation with skilled wicce often becoming revered as priestesses and priests of whichever the current dominant religion happened to be, even to the point of deification themselves. However, as religions became institutions, increasingly seduced by their own power and egoic delusions, they began to hoard magic to themselves and recast the wicce as demonic. Magic, such as turning bread and wine into flesh and blood, a magical transformation effected for centuries by the pre-Christian cults of Osiris and Mithras, became the rituals and rites of the Church alone. Any magic affected without the Church was recast as demonic witchery, cleverly ensuring that power did not stray from the institution.

That which was once an almost ordinary experience to our ancient sisters and brothers became 'miraculous' rather than magical, a subtle yet powerful shift of terminology pushing magic even further away from the general population. Religion had successfully appropriated magical practices and the Otherworld as their own, hence our embedded assumption that religion and magical practice are equivalent.

The result is that today Paganism is the religion and leading companion for witchcraft, even to the point that the terms 'witchcraft' and 'paganism' are used interchangeably. Nonetheless there are Christian, Pagan, Mormon, Atheist, Heathen witches and more. Religion certainly blends well with witchcraft in its ultimate acknowledgment of a super-natural element to life, yet the extent to which major faiths have borrowed and appropriated extremely heavily from the ancient Craft is a fact most good Christian folk would rather ignore.

It is time however, for witches to ignore it no longer and to identify that not only has Christianity appropriated from the Craft, but that witchcraft has appropriated materials in return. In attempting to clarify this complex relationship between religion and the Craft I do not mean to suggest that it is possible, or even desirable to attempt to take the religion out of witchcraft. It is desirable however; to be aware that we are making a choice to include religious elements and concepts in our work, and that any such a choice will necessarily situate our magic within the limitations of human thought and expectation. Often of course, this is exactly what is required.

There is one further distinction to be made between the religious and scientific nature of magic, which I hope will highlight further the importance of truly understanding the implications of assuming witchcraft to be necessarily religious. The scientific or shamanic magic of the natural world exists *a priori,* meaning that it pre-dates and is a pre-condition of, our human experience. The cosmological principles of the energetic, interconnected natural world existed long before the human constructs which we use to categorise, order and limit our world came into existence. Anthropologists commonly understand that shamanic practices were once a human-wide natural way of engaging with the ancient world, and every single society on Earth despite their culture, beliefs, religions and social norms can trace magical practices back to a common shamanic seed.

The religious magic, which refers to any tradition which prizes hierarchy, dogma and the controlling disposition of human 'power,' has moved away from natural laws which exist *a priori* or before, humanity. Religious magic, which was performed in the classical world became the noble way practiced by Kings and gentry who were able to read, write and prized reason above all. This classical world was still Pagan however, which demonstrates that it doesn't matter which religion is practiced, when religion comes first, be it pantheistic or monotheistic, Pagan or Christian then religion dominates and the natural order diminishes. Religious magic is closer therefore to human psychology and society than shamanic witchcraft which exists alongside the pre-human natural order of the universe, and an area in the modern Craft where this difference is most marked is within initiations.

In chapter five you will read of two wicce initiation rites. Although these ceremonies contain structural and ritualistic observances, their aim is not to ally the candidate to a specific group or to immerse them within any one tradition. The focus of wicce initiations is to enable the initiate, with the aid of their spirit guides, to become director of their own spiritual journey and development. To this end, initiations become increasingly spontaneous, incorporating materials offered or intuited within the moment of fervour. You will see for example, that within the second initiation rite presented in chapter five, how the candidate experiences a soul retrieval however, another candidate may not require any parts of their soul to be recovered and their second initiation may involve an entirely different experience altogether.

Each initiation from the introductory to the third ritual contains some scope for specific direction from the candidate's spiritual guides, with the leader/facilitator of the ritual always attentive therefore to each individual, guiding them as appropriate, keeping an open mind and acknowledging the need for some spontaneity. Although the first introductory initiation contains little opportunity for this as it is a formality rather anything else, the initiations increase in their esoteric significance requiring greater efficacy of personal spiritual involvement.

In this way, initiations always allow for both spiritual and conscious evolution for the candidate and the Craft in general. Ideally therefore, wicce initiations aim for a balance between fluid natural magic and ritual structure with its embedded societal principles, a balance which reflects the meeting of human and divine will within an integrated self. Passion and reason become a unity, and this unity is the state of a fully developed ego which no longer turns to fear as a measure for life.

It is regrettable that a number of modern magical groups provide only psychological initiatory experiences which isolate the ego, causing it to dwell within its own illusions. Initiations which fall into this category of magic can still be quite the experience, yet they are imposed from the outside with elaborate ritual, regalia and even shock tactics. This sometimes pantomime approach has risen in popularity today as it requires little of the candidate beyond their psychological susceptibility, rather than any real psychic or spiritual abilities. Such initiations are specifically designed to be visually and experientially impressive, to make an indelible sensory and psychological mark upon the candidate, and it is now known within psychology how we tend to remember and give greater value to those experiences which are imprinted upon our memories in vivid sensory or emotional forms.

Strong memories are created with adrenaline which acts as a kind of mental setting agent. The stronger the emotion or sensory experience at the time, the more adrenaline is released and the more enduring and powerful the memory becomes. This power then gives us the illusion that a particular memory is more valuable than others, whether that memory is positive or negative does not matter, we will still afford it greater significance in our lives returning to it again and again believing it to be formative of who we are. The reality is however, it is just a memory. It is just a thought which will only continue to affect us if we give it energy.

Unfortunately, the stronger the memory, the greater the power we afford it without realising that this is a symptom not of a wonderful magical experience, a flowing of energy but rather, a stagnant experience which continues to drain and bind our energy to it, and often to the group involved for the rest of our lives. Even good memories can become stagnant, draining and unhealthily obsessive, limiting our future expectations and assumptions regarding what the world 'should' be like. Esoteric initiations however, work beyond the realms of just psychological and emotional effect. This is not to imply that psychology and emotion are somehow removed from esoteric rites, not at all, rather, they assume their appropriate significance as energetic constructs of our experience without which, we could not integrate the ritual into our physical consciousness. Psychology and emotion help to navigate and interpret our experiences, being the structure not the goal of the encounter.

When energy flows without blockages magic happens. It is the breath of the universe. When the movement is large, beyond our current understanding of what is possible we now call it a miracle. Instantaneous healings, walking on water, turning water into wine and making more of less is just the flowing of energy directed by a skilled Craft worker, who has recognised that he/she is the same as the movement rather than being in control of anything. We can enter into the web of wyrd which is woven moment by moment by the three sisters seated beneath the world tree, and become the intent of each emerging moment rather than seeking to command, manipulate or beg the sisters to weave a certain outcome. We can become the magic we seek because we are the magic we seek.

Even modern empirical scientists are beginning to speculate that there is an energy like consciousness, which may pervade the whole universe. Remember how physics has discovered that particles have a vibrational core rather than being solid matter? Well even more amazing is that when a particle is split into two halves and one half is isolated at some distance from the other, then what is done to one half happens instantaneously to the other. This should be impossible. Nothing, so we thought, could move that fast. How did the other half of the particle receive the information that something had happened to its partner so quickly, faster even than the speed of light?

Einstein himself had speculated that he believed there was 'something' which could travel faster than the speed of light, although he had no idea what it could be. Today, increasing numbers of physicists are speculating that a consciousness links everything together like a giant web, allowing information to pass immediately through the web of creation regardless of space and time. So science is finally catching up with what the wicce knew hundreds of years ago, having learnt it from their direct experience of the magical world.

ᛈ

5. DIARY OF A SHAMANIC WITCH

What follows are the semi-fictional diary extracts from a new wicce joining a traditional tribe of witches for the first time. Her magical name is Raven and the extracts are taken from Yule, Imbolc, Beltain and Samhain celebrations as well as a general evening of instruction. Two of these feast days mark Raven's first two initiation rites. This is the ancient Craft of the wicce, the way of wiccecræft as it survives today complete with its spontaneity, its story-telling, poetry and magic.

The large paragraphs of OE included in this chapter are from the 'nine herbs charm' which appears in the Lacnunga manuscript. This is perhaps the most mysterious and enigmatically tantalising charm/spell/initiation which has ever been recorded, in fact it is most likely the only initiation rite ever recorded from our ancient past and is thought to be far older than the manuscript itself. It is obvious however, that it has not been recorded in its entirety and although little Christianisation occurs, it appears that much of the heathen direction has simply been left out instead. Nonetheless, this chapter aims to offer an insight into how the old ways discussed within these pages may live to inspire modern witches. Welcome to the tribe of Andredswold!

1- Yule (1ˢᵗ Initiation or principle rite of passage)

I've been awake for over twenty four hours yet I still feel filled with elation and energy like everything is different and new. I just don't want to go to sleep in case I awaken without this feeling and I wish I had the gift of poeticism to bring forth words rich enough to describe it, so even when normal life resumes I could always open these pages and remember. I could write of beauty, truth and light but I would still remain frustratingly short of even an adequate description, so I must somehow find 'good enough' words to cast a shadow of my experience as shadows seem as close as words can get for one as unskilled with them as I. So let me attempt.

It's like everything is the same yet looks altered, like my eyes are taking in more light and my senses are clearer, purer and more acute. The green of the grass is greener than it is meant to be and the song of the Robin more fluent. I sense the fatigue within my body whilst equally knowing that I am not my body but another more ethereal type of being enjoying the ride. I don't want to go sleep and awaken again to the seriousness of the minutia of life. I do not want to be drowned in the mundane, to feel it sucking at me with its lists of 'should's' and 'ought's' and 'should not's'. I want to always remember who I am, a joyous being flowing into the physical world full of curiosity and wonder never taking it too seriously, personally or literally. Before the inevitable returns however, and mundane life takes its grip once more, I will record as much of last night's events as I can possibly recall.

Yesterday I took the first rite of passage into an older more traditional form of the Craft than the witchcraft I have tried before. Its style is shamanic drawing on a real lineage of experience which thankfully, still survives. It's a bit weird that it's not a coven. I'm so used to the idea of witches being in covens but I guess this is a relatively modern idea, modern for witchcraft anyway. To be a tribe (*mægþ*) emphasises the community orientation of this *wiccecræft* which reflects an era earlier than the burning times when witches did not need to skulk about in secret meetings. Yesterday therefore, I joined the tribe of Andredswold. Some tribes call themselves *inhired* which is a masculine Old English word for family but we prefer the feminine word for tribe *mægþ* in honour of the great warrior Goddess Andred who is our patron. We are a family too but always tribe, earthy, fiery, active and enthused.

It's taken nine months for me to reach this point and what a nine months it has been. I have always wanted to be part of something real, primal and magical yet it has taken me years to finally find a group which feels like home. From the moment I met Sophie, there it was, recognition, I felt it acutely like a wrench deep in my stomach which drew me forwards. At my first full moon meeting I realised that we were a family, not tied by blood but by something even more enduring. We were all there due to a deep honouring of the Earth and all her children from the tiniest plants to the most egocentric manifestations of humanity. We are all the same.

The tribe has a hierarchy but not one that encourages one person to have control over all the others. All matters are decided by a group of *ealdors* who have worked within the Craft for years. *Ealdors* are only ever invited to the position when certain signs have occurred directing a tribesperson's elevation. The leader of the tribe (*ricenn*) is never an *ealdor* and the *ealdors* appoint a different *ricenn* (a female endowed with the attributes of the goddess) every three years. At the moment however, there aren't enough female members of experience and so Sophie is standing in as *ricenn* until one of the newer members is ready for the position.

I arrived at Sophie's (*Æthelfrith*- her magical name in Old English) at about nine yesterday morning armed with my rucksack, boots, matches, really warm clothes and a packed lunch of rice, fruit and bottled water as requested. I had speculated endlessly about what may happen. I was right about being outside and alone for hours but that was as far my rationalising succeeded. I parked my car in the gravel driveway and knocked at the large oak door. Sophie greeted me with her usual hug and pressed into my hand a small stone covered in runic inscriptions which I was told to keep with me for the rest of the day and night. I was then instructed to follow the path at the side of the house down into the woodland and to stay there and not to return until the sun begins to set but to return by the same path.

I had journeyed this path before. The field by the house is meadowland with a winding route mowed within it leading to a small brook before the boundary of woodland trees begins. Some months earlier I had been formally welcomed to the group as a *féðegest*, a traveller journeying the lands, resting awhile with the tribe. Sophie's husband had mowed a great labyrinth into the meadow back then and I had walked with a lamp to its centre where the *ealdors* were awaiting me.

Whilst seated on the grass at the centre of the maze the *ealdors* each asked me a question. I can't remember all their questions but one was "where have you travelled from sister?" and another, "what do you seek?" I also remember being asked about the obstacles I had met on my path so far and how I had overcome them and if I felt I had overcome them successfully. Stuff like that. When each *ealdor* had asked their question they sat quietly for some time. Apparently they are able to meet and discuss things on another plane and I think that's what they were doing, discussing me in the ethers! I let my mind drift and after some time heard the soft beat of a drum calling the other members into the centre of the labyrinth. Then more drums joined in with singing and shouting as the tribe came nearer and the air of solemnity changed into a celebration with food, wine and storytelling into the early hours.

This time the path was more direct leading me to the line of trees marking the boundary of the woodland. Entering the stark wood devoid of much of its foliage I felt rather bereft and alone. It was a cold day and the air was filled with the possibility of early snowfall. I decided to find a sheltered spot and see if I could make a small fire of my own, otherwise, I would freeze despite my warm clothes. I knew Sophie stored wood in a small shed somewhere near the edge of the forest and hoped it was the right thing to do to raid some of the dry logs there. I had been told to bring matches so surely I was expected to make a fire?

After a small time searching I happened across the small weather board shed, dug a pit into the dry earth and laid a small fire. Some bark scrapings sufficed as kindling and invoking my Girl Guide spirit within, I set to work. I asked the elementals of fire to join me and lend their strength and light to my journey and sure enough, within minutes the welcome dancing of fiery sprites warmed my hands. As the flames took hold I built the fire up further with logs and watched as its heart glowed and breathed. And there I stayed for the next seven hours.

It was strange having nothing to do but be. I had quietened my mind before, meditating, trying to achieve what the Buddhists call mindfulness but only now could I appreciate how, when I had previously thought I was successfully focused I was in fact busy fighting my constant mental chatter. Always, lurking at the back of my mind, just beyond the edge of my own denial were the thoughts and personal reprimands- 'you still need to do the dishes, change the cat's litter, prepare that seminar for tomorrow, do some weeding!' etc etc. I may not have been actively thinking about these things whilst meditating but the energy was always with me, it's a hard thing to explain. Sitting by that fire however, having absolutely nothing else to do, similar mental spectres began to haunt me in their accustomed way.

At first there were a multitude of thoughts and memories. Past regrets, loads of those. I had to struggle really hard not to spend the whole day just beating myself over the head with a torrent of the past which I could do nothing to change anyway. I felt the heavy energy of long held regrets, angst's and shames and it took all my attention and desire to breathe them out, asking Mother Earth to absorb them and cleanse them. After some time, the darkness lifted and my mind became tranquil.

I sank into the earth, at least that's how it felt. It was release, lightness, beauty, and that's when the tears flowed. How much do I hold onto? Why? The world of things, places to be, functions to perform and worries to contemplate endlessly, just disappeared in the bird song, the crackling of the fire and the peace of that existing. I ate rice, drank water and lived more in that day of apparent nothingness than I had ever lived in the whole of my life. My work, my favourite clothes, the accumulation of stuff seemed as shadows to me, a half life. It was both a powerful and humbling experience. Hours passed in being and living and as the sun began to dip I thanked the fire spirits for their help and bade them farewell before returning to the meadow.

I walked with increasing anticipation. I had undergone initiations before having once been a member of a high magical order. I remember being really really nervous before those initiations though, not knowing what on earth was going to happen. I felt completely different this time however. There was obviously some trepidation, are we ever truly fearless of the unknown future? Perhaps some are that fearless, that secure, the Byron Katie's of this world perhaps, but unfortunately I'm not yet that spiritually enlightened.

My mind shot back to the dark temple of the magical order, heavy with exotic incense. My heart would pound away in my chest as I was hoodwinked and led to the temple door. The rituals were always extremely elaborate and intensely experiential; I will certainly never forget them!

This time however, the smell of the earth and the evensong of birds all carried me towards an energy far more ancient. My heart wasn't pounding with nerves it was beating with the sound of drums now reaching me from the sacred space. Pulsing, beating, living.

Æthelfrith met me at the path's end, I saw her lantern swaying in the gentle but chilly breeze and taking her outstretched hand we walked together the rest of the way. We turned left at the house moving on into the sacred space where the sweat lodge and stone circle (a modern one) were enclosed by a small clump of trees. It was almost dark when we entered the clump and little was visible although I could make out the shapes of people. A glow emerged from the interior of the sweat lodge and it was to this that I was led. Sophie told me to go into the lodge where I would find a change of clothes. After I had changed I was to extinguish the candle and await the opening of the door. When the door was opened I should emerge. Sounded simple enough.

I slithered down into the earthen structure. The sweat lodge is sunken into the ground with a seat stretching around the wall made from the earth herself with a roof of willow covered in tarpaulin. As the hatch closed behind me my eyes took in the glowing stones of the fire pit which were warm rather than roasting giving the interior a cosy womblike feel. And there it was, my woollen robe. It was rich brown and thickly lined against winter's creeping cold. I changed eagerly although kept my thermals and boots on before extinguishing the candle to be wrapped in a fiery glow once more. A faint drumming reached my ears, a heartbeat lulling me into a sleepy reverie. The tribe were conducting the Yule (*Geola*) celebrations. I drifted in and out of awareness with only the chant standing out due to its repetition:

"By fire and by water, between the earth and sky, we stand like the World Tree, rooted deep and crowned high!"

When the hatch was opened I had no idea how much time had passed. At first I hadn't wanted to move, it was so comfortable in the womb of earth and I heard strange sounds from outside which caused me to wonder for a moment whether staying inside would be a better idea. There was a moaning, almost wailing and as I looked out of the lodge suddenly everything appeared unfamiliar. There seemed to be a darkened tunnel although I could make out a light beyond, somewhere in the distance.

A smell wafted over to me, it was a cooking smell, really enticing as I felt my stomach respond with a desirous wanting after the meagre day of rice and fruit. I was lured out by my groaning tummy, emerging from the lodge on all fours, cautious of the darkened tunnel which was writhing, moaning, everything was moving, vibrating and I felt scared at first before I realised the tunnel was made from the legs of the tribe. They were standing, legs apart in a long line, waving to and fro.

The scene reminds me now of an account I once read of a young monk travelling through the thickly forested east of England during the fifteenth century. One dark night, on the outskirts of a small sea-side village he heard sounds from the shore and ventured to investigate. He tells of witnessing a group of women standing just as my tribeswomen were standing, legs apart in a long line whilst another woman crawled from a cave through their legs and out toward a fire burning upon the sand.

The young monk describes the scene in reverent terms as he realises he is witnessing an ancient rite of initiation which few eyes would ever have beheld. How ancient such a rite truly is can be little more than speculation, however, there is a fascinating similarity between this and a depiction discovered in a 13,000 year old English cave painting. The natural formation of Creswell Crags in Nottinghamshire astounded archaeologists when they discovered cave art which displays a line of women described as apparently dancing in some sort of conga line. There is no way the ancient painters would have depicted such a thing in such a sacred place unless it was important. The similarity between the line of dancing women in the cave, the line of swaying women on the beach and my fellow tribeswomen who, if captured in relief would certainly appear to be dancing, is amazingly thought provoking.

The grass beneath my hands was damp as I crawled forward towards the light. I emerged into the arms of *Æthelfrith* and her husband who wrapped me in a large blanket and drew me to the fire where I sat gratefully, recovering from the disorientation and jelly like feeling in my legs. The drum beat continued and soon *Æthelfrith* lifted me *"you must now meet the nygon sweostars* (nine sisters)" she said, leading me to the first stone of the great circle. Standing before each stone was a member of the tribe and as I passed to each I was directed to look at one of the symbols inscribed upon the stone which I had been given many hours before.

Each symbol represented one of the original nine wicce sisters, created in the flowing of wyrd. Each whispered to me as I passed *"honour your ancestors", "honour the earth", "be led from your heart", "have compassion for all", "what is inside is outside", "perception is fluid", "thought divides",* those are the ones I remember now. I then walked around twice more unguided as the tribe moved towards the fire, settling themselves in a circle around the flames. The drum beat guided my pace and the mysterious chant calmed my soul: *"Her com ingangan inwriðen with, his haman on handa, legde þe his teage on sweoran, on gunnan him of þæm lande".*

When my journey of three circles was complete *Æthelfrith* stepped forward to bring me to the centre of the sacred space where another *ealdor* stood waiting.

"Who have you brought before us?" he asked.

"A child of the Earth, a child of the Sun and a child of the Moon" *Æthelfrith* replied.

"and how can we know her?"

"we can look upon her and know her"

"And by what name shall she be called?"

"call her by her name, Raven"

"Folk of Andredswold, look upon Raven and know her as our own, may the Gods protect, guide and inspire her."

Then I had to say the oath which I had memorised:

"I thank you for honouring me with this hospitality and welcome, and I vow to honour you and the tribe in return. I will always keep to my heart what occurs of intimate natures and respect you all and hold you dear. If at any point I feel I cannot continue in this journey then I swear to always honour this oath to you as I bid my leave and journey to other kingdoms."

I was then duly welcomed:

"Welcome Raven, to the tribe of Andredswold. Share our meal and drink mead with us, we are brothers and sisters."

Everyone cheered and came to offer their greetings before attentions immediately turned to the cauldron which was bubbling and gurgling with thick stew. My stomach joined the gurgling! Wooden bowls were quickly filled and passed around the circle. I shared my first meal with the tribe as a full member, an important event, the sharing of what we have, right from the beginning. It's a symbol of equality and mutual respect. Some may be further advanced in the tribe than others but this is just part of the journey. Advancement demands greater sacrifice with more responsibility rather than commanding more power of domination which we commonly assume to be the case from modern experiences. If ever an *ealdor* or *thegn* (those who have taken the third rite) appear to be allowing their ego to become confused then some sort of intervention apparently occurs to guide them otherwise. Everything is done through the council of *ealdors,* no one person has 'control'.

The hot stew was so very welcome along with sweet tea and then a glass of mulled wine. I felt exhilarated. I still feel exhilarated, liberated too. There is a freedom in this path, a freedom of spirit and self.

2- Imbolc (Earth healing ceremony)

Today's feast of fire was dedicated to healing the Earth and all her children. Unfortunately, as we began to arrive at Sophie's the weather was far from fiery as buckets of rain threw themselves down from dark grey clouds. Those collecting wood for the fire would have a hard time and I suspected that Sophie's secret stash of dry logs would need to be raided again. I must admit to being rather relieved that my duty was in the kitchen. Normally I preferred to be outside doing the wood, collecting herbs or preparing the sacred space but the warmth of the Aga was far more comforting and I watched with a mixture of compassion but relief as the rain hammered against the leaded glass of the window.

When the rain falls or the wind howls, which is common in England, Sophie always waxes lyrical about building a real meeting hall of mud, wood and thatch if only the local planning department would allow it. One day she vows, they will acquiesce but until then we make do with a large tent like structure which has been specifically modelled and made to fit about the stone circle and elevated in the centre by a large wooded support. As the evening drew in however, the rain became less persistent, retreating to the north in search of London and a more urban night life to disrupt. We didn't need the tent after all.

Ensconced by the Aga, I was on potato duty. A mound of white fleshy tubas stood before me and as I peeled potato after potato I stared in disbelief as the mound stayed the same size, or so it certainly appeared. I am no cook, my potatoes I'm afraid to admit usually come in a packet, pre-prepared to put straight in the oven. Over the past couple of months I have tried to slowly change my habits and use more fresh foods to gain a greater respect and connection with what I am eating. I've started using frozen peas instead of tinned! Whether I will ever get as far as actually growing my own like Sophie and James I don't know. One thing is for certain, I now know how to peel and cook real potatoes so that is one small step at least.

I watched as Ben (*Garberend*), a brother of the second rite, tipped garlic, onion, herbs and cubes of lamb into the cauldron which would be taken out to the fire at the last minute to finish its cooking. We then prepared flasks of hot tea and carried them out of the kitchen door and into the creeping darkness. The moon had emerged from the clouds which were heading for London leaving a clear, cold, star filled night. Soon the flames of the sacred space became visible and we headed there with our offerings.

Great torches circled the grove illuminating the standing stones casting long shadows which disappeared back into darkness. A great fire roared in the centre warming everyone who had worked on the outside preparations and fire mandalas were staked into the gaps between the stones at each quarter, a different symbol for each element with a small alter assembled around each blazing mandala. In the north was a bowl of fruits and nuts representing renewal and in the east was a mass of green foliage for rebirth. Blue was the colour of the west for spiritual insight and yellow for the south and the Sun God of light. Smaller candles secured in lanterns circled the edge of the sacred space representing all the peoples and living beings of Earth.

When all was prepared and hot tea had been welcomed with eager hands we returned to the house to change into heavy robes complete with gloves, hoods and scarves. As the evening progressed the latter garments were discarded as bodies became hot from dancing. Sophie had headed out before us and when she was ready she called the tribe forward with the moaning sounds of the deep *cúhorn* (a musical horn made from the horn of a cow). We walked in line from the familiar domesticity of the kitchen towards the avenue of torches which led into the clump of trees and the sacred space. We entered in silence as *Æthelfrith* stood, staff in hand in the centre of the circle, swaying gently, lips moving with hushed hidden words. *Brandon*, a brother of the third rite threw handfuls of aromatic herbs upon the fire and its charcoal embers glowed brilliant orange and red from deep within. Our sister Sarah (*Cwenhild*- who we all think will be made *ricenn* soon) took up the lantern before her and began to walk sunwise (deosil), slowly around the outside of the stones saying:

"I carry this flame of light around this sacred place and ask that all spirits depart unless invited. I welcome the great elements of balance to ward this place and I welcome the Goddess Brighid to our meeting that she may bring forth life and light from her womb to sustain the earth. All hail!"

Cwenhild rejoined the circle of tribe members as we all turned our focus to *Æthelfrith* still standing with her arms outstretched, staff aloft who said in a deep and sonorous voice:

"Hear us ancient ones, witnesses of eternity, holders of the key, we are gathered before you we creatures of the earth and heavens in the name of the great goddess Brighid, pregnant mother, renewer of life on Earth to ask that the door between the worlds may be opened for healing to flow."

Æthelfrith brought down her staff to the earth and knocked three times upon the ground. Softly chanting she began to sway, eyes closed. The tribe becoming one body followed her motions, bodies moved gently at first then feet stepped in time to the chant which was now taken by all:

"Earth my body, Water my blood, Air my breath and Fire my spirit!"

The chant was familiar to me from years of experimenting in Wiccan covens. I was thankful it was in modern English too! I love to hear the spoken Old English of course, it is a lovely language, powerful and poetic but I am still far from mastering it. Not all tribes demand the use of Old English but as Sophie is a scholar of Anglo-Saxon England it is a wonderful opportunity for us to learn the old ways in all their glory.

I followed the tribe's steps which grew into a circle dance, round and round left foot to the side and right in front, left to the side and right in front, faster and faster we went with drum beat insistent compelling us round. Soon the circle became wild. We left the regular pattern behind and whirled and stomped in our frenzied peculiar ways, arms waved up then down, some crouched and others stretched as the dancing took hold. Gloves were thrown off and woolly hats discarded, fire roared and voices flew. Earth, air, fire, water were vibrating with magic and spirit until *Æthelfrith* raised her arms once more bringing us all to a sudden halt with raised arms and linked hands, holding the energy with her to its crucial point:

"The door has been opened and we speak and dance for the peoples of Earth when we send this energy out on the wings of our great Mother who bore us all." The staff shot into the air as gathered energy soared out and around the globe to all those in need be they plants, animals, rocks or people. *Brighid* could now give birth within a fertile and healthy world.

We all collapsed on the ground suddenly exhausted but happy and content. An owl swooped down from the trees and flew about us, a good omen that our work was well done. There was a small flurry of activity as food became the next priority on the agenda. We were famished! Ben was already on the case having slipped out quickly to bring the heavy cauldron back to the circle and mounting it upon the iron support which had miraculously appeared from behind a stone. We thanked the Goddess for her bounty before passing out the bowls and devouring the whole lamb stew in lightening speed followed by intense chocolate cake made by *Garberend's* own fair but large hands and all was washed down by quite large amounts of mead and wine.

With appetites satisfied the atmosphere became relaxed and easy. The fire glowed with heat and occasional flame as *Pendragon* (James, Sophie's husband) motioned for quiet. Slumped round the fire, pulling blankets around us we sipped at our glasses while *Pendragon* began the story of *Sé græg docga* (The grey dog). The tale tells of *Wulf,* an Anglo-Saxon of the first generation. His parents had sailed from the old lands when he was small bringing the old Gods with them into this new land of fertile soil. During his life time this new country of *Engaland* was turned away from the old Gods towards the nailed God of foreigners from over the southern waters.

The nailed God was harsh commanding suffering, penance and obedience from his followers. Worship of the old ones was forbidden yet during a particularly harsh winter *Wulf's* thoughts turned to the Valkyrie Goddess *Rheda* who had protected their lands during the cold season for millennia and whose sacred spring still bubbled from the earth nearby. Although dedicated to the new Saint Anne, *Wulf* knew the great *Rheda* had not deserted them.

Wulf knew they needed *Rheda's* help if they were to survive the winter. The local *Thegn* (overlord) had become greedy desiring everything he could find to increase his wealth and power leaving the common folk with little. Unfortunately, adding to the people's worries, *Wulf's* dog called Bonecruncher who had a fearsome reputation for fighting off hungry wolves, had become coveted by the *Thegn*.

The local village could not survive the winter without

Bonecruncher to ward off the wolves attacks and so *Wulf* set out to seek the ancient *Rheda's* intervention to keep Bonecruncher safe from the desires of the *Thegn*. *Wulf* decided, under cover of dawn's mist to visit the great Goddess once again.

Arriving at her ancient spring he set out his offerings of flour, beans and wool before sitting quietly, allowing his mind to drift. When peaceful and focused *Wulf* began to imagine a deep pool beneath the spring where his prayer to the Goddess would be received. He sang his prayer intently, seeing it drawn down into the darkness where the Goddess would find it and cause it to take form. After sending his prayer *Wulf* stood up and as he did so his cloak fell apart, slithered off his shoulders and sank into *Rheda's* dark pool. *Wulf* was greatly saddened thinking this to be a bad omen, perhaps the Goddess was angry with him for converting to Christianity?

He walked home with the soaking wet cloak in his arms feeling frozen to the bone. Reaching his small home he hung the cloak from a wooden strut and went to sleep awakening the following morning to the sound his father shouting Bonecruncher's name. *Wulf* leapt from his bed, horrified that something may have happened to the dog so soon but as he reached for his cloak a strange dizzying feeling came over him. It seemed as if the cloak was not quite real, its edges were blurred and as he reached for it his hand met air. *Wulf* shock his head, sure he was still half asleep and when he grabbed for the cloak once more he felt its damp material and pulled it over his shoulders.

Once outside *Wulf* took his father's arm to calm him as he suddenly realised that for some strange reason he knew exactly where the dog was. *Wulf* ran through the snow to the nearby trees just as he heard the shouts and hooves of the *Thegn* approaching in the distance. In the bracken *Wulf* found Bonecruncher, the dog was safe but startled when *Wulf* grabbed at his grey fur and pulled him to the ground throwing the cloak over both their bodies just as the *Thegn* came into view. At that moment *Wulf* knew that *Rheda* had indeed granted his prayer. Even though the *Thegn* was looking straight at them, the cloak, still damp with the water from *Rheda's* spring made them invisible to his greed so Bonecruncher remained in the village protecting it from the winter wolves.

The tribe cheered when *Pendragon* finished his tale. More mead flowed, songs were sung and other tales told until cold took hold and it was time for *Æthelfrith* to stand once more, staff raised and ask for the door between worlds to now be closed and for all who had aided us to return to their dwellings in peace.

Bael (Healing ritual)

It has been a very long day. I rose early to greet the great sun as he broke the horizon with rays of gold. I have risen with him every year on this day for the past twenty years except for a couple of times when the early summer flu has forced me into retreat beneath my duvet. This morning however, I felt healthy and alive (although still thick with sleep) as I walked the ten minutes it takes from my house to the village where I met with the Morris Men for the usual May Day celebrations which still occur every year even in the congested south east of England. Come rain or shine, I play the drum and flute for the Morris dancing, welcoming the sun and marking what would once have been the beginning of a whole day of festivities and celebrations. Unfortunately, our village no longer dances the maypole or crowns a May Queen with garlands of flowers, the only signs that such traditions were once kept is the name of the small lane which runs from the high street beyond the Church, 'Maypole Lane'.

We danced and made merry for about an hour and would have continued far longer had we not been forced to retreat from the first signs of traffic hooting their horns at us as they attempted to get an early start to wherever they were eager to go. We withdrew graciously and contentedly into the local pub situated by the Church which always opens early for us with hot tea and full English. I love this day! For just one hour out of every year villagers come together to celebrate the beginning of summer on the same spot where villagers have conducted their festivals for years. In that one hour from sunrise we reclaim our relationship with the land, the sky and each other before cars swamp us once more, reminding us of just how congested, fraught and over-populated our world has become.

With a full stomach I returned home for a few hours before going to Sophie's. She and James only live about twenty minutes drive away in another small village which also bears witness to the past with its name 'Mayfield'. There is still an ancient sacred spring at Mayfield although it is now enclosed by a small wooden construction and owned by the Church who lock the doors of the ancient shrine and use the sacred place as a storage room for chairs, tables and the like.

I arrived at their house around two o'clock along with the others and we began with the usual tea, biscuits and much catching up. Appetites satisfied Sarah went over what we needed to do. We were to collect herbs, lavender, vervain, St John's wort and chamomile to make a small pouch or a poppet, which ever we chose. It was a wonderfully sunny day and knowing now where Sophie's herbs were to be found we set out together into the garden, enjoying the sunshine.

We sat in the courtyard herb garden which was such a sun trap that most herbs flowered there far sooner than in other gardens. Most of us had chosen to make little poppets. We asked permission for each herb and grass we plucked and wove the herbs and grasses into small corn-dolly like figurines to represent ourselves.

Mine was about two inches in height and compact with fairy foxglove hair. Louise had used daisy heads to make two huge breasts which caused much amusement as we sat in the sun weaving away, grass over stem, over grass over stem holding in our minds something of ourselves which we wished to be released from. It was such a perfect afternoon and when our poppets were made our thoughts turned to the next part of our preparations, decorating the sacred space with garlands and greenery. I made a display of marigold and early chamomile, both of which could be taken home by us all after the celebrations and used in our herbal concoctions. Sarah made her head garland, others collected the fire wood and lots of it whilst James took kitchen duty.

When all preparations were made and the sun was considering its decent we formed a procession complete with drums, bells, water, garlands, candles and petals and wove our way to the sacred space where Sarah/*Cwenhild* was waiting. She marked our foreheads with blessed water as we entered the clump of trees to a marvellous sight of fruits, flowers, oak and ash boughs, and torches. When we were all within, the great central fire was lit. It was larger than normal, not quite a bonfire but not far off.

We continued to walk sunwise around the stones tracing a circle with fire, petals and blessed water. Three times we circled with our familiar chant *"Blessed be this sacred ground as we stride once, twice, thrice around."* As we came to rest *Cwenhild* raised her staff high and sang clearly *"Great Goddess Freyja, Queen of the forest, Seer of the waters, we celebrate and rejoice with you on this first day of summer. Oh blessed Lady of Asgard, valkyrie warrior residing over the cycles of life and death, wild woman of the north we raise our voices in your honour!"* we all joined in with *"dóméadig Freyja!"* (Blessed Freya) three times. Aromatic herbs were cast to the fire and other offerings of fruits, cake and wine were placed for the Goddess upon the hearth.

Cwenhild then led us through an elemental balancing visualisation to prepare us for the magical transformations which were about to occur. Turning to the final rays of the setting sun we felt the masculine energy unite with us flowing into our core, we raised our arms to the west and felt the energy surge in through our fingertips. Then, following *Cwenhild's* lead we slowly sank onto one knee whilst drawing the energy down and over us too. Standing again we turned to the large bowl of water which represented the sacred spring beneath *Yggdrasill* the world tree and repeated the process of drawing the energy, this time of water, into and over us, feeling it combining with our energy. We continued likewise for earth and air.

Once we had balanced and infused our energy with the four elements the drumming started. Just a slow heartbeat at first whilst *Cwenhild* focused upon raising the song. She began in the sing song lilt of Old English *"Hieran ús Freyja, onhyrdan uré módsefa"*.

We started to sway and dance to the quickening beat with song soaring and weaving, as sisters and brothers created harmony in a round. We performed a circle dance we had learned from one of Sophie's workshops and stomped with belled ankles to and fro round and around, laughing, singing, building pace, heating bodies and creating energy until at some point within the frenzy we stopped, breathing hard to see *Cwenhild* with arms raised holding the energy which was to be directed into our poppets of herbs and flowers. Each of us had secured our small selves carefully within our robes for the correct time and reached for them now.

I held mine before me and concentrated on the one thing I truly wished to transform in my life. I let the thoughts and emotions take form within her, cradled in her scented limbs. Pressing her warm body to my forehead I imagined all the fear which blocks my spirit surge into her and when I felt a release I thanked her, wished her well and cast her to the waiting flames. One by one poppets were consumed by fire transforming or releasing the blocks we had focused on. A sense of relief and then new life surged over me as energy started to flow once more in regions which had been starved and blocked for maybe thirty or more years. Sophie had told me that this ceremony would be a significant point on my journey from the first to the second rite.

Samhain (2nd Initiation- the main rite of passage)

I fasted the whole of yesterday in preparation for the evening ritual. This was the 'big one'. If the first rite had been about rebirth then this was certainly about coming of age. It wasn't just a marker of adulthood though, it was a full exorcism of the old demons holding me back and a re-centring, like a higher rebirth yet again of my new self. This is the stage of the wicce proper. Do I feel different? Yes! How? Can't quite say!

My day started early in rubber boots and anorak whilst clutched in my hand was a detailed list of nine herbs which I was to gather and take with me to the ritual. I was suddenly glad of the past months of intense herb lore lessons from Sophie as I felt quite confident about how and when to collect each herb. Not all were directly available from garden or hedgerow during the autumn so I had certain dried herbs and oils standing by. I needed mugwort, plantain, chamomile, apple, fennel, chervil, black nightshade, nettle, and lamb's cress. I had no idea why I needed them but I foraged the farm track behind my house nonetheless feeling that great sense of freedom one only really gets from being outside in the elements.

Since my first rite I had established a small herb garden outside my kitchen window although more vigorous varieties were literally 'contained' in my terracotta pots. The mint had become especially rampant earlier this year requiring stern measures as it had attempted to strangle the sage and feverfew nestling beside it with a dignity certainly not shared by the mint!

I already had the fennel, mugwort, plantain, chamomile, chervil and apple stored from earlier in the year. I foraged for black nightshade which, as we have had a late autumn was still to be found along the hedge row. I still felt rather cautious about picking this herb, it's so similar to its deadly sister that doubt welled up in my mind with its entertaining visual accompaniments of me dying in agony, hands clutching my stomach with the tribal *ealdors* shaking their heads muttering that I obviously wasn't ready for this honour after all.

I pulled a picture from the internet out of the pocket of my jeans and examined the depiction of the black nightshade carefully, then the plant in front of me and then a second illustration from the internet. I was taking no chances. I finally plucked up the confidence to pick the nightshade and then turned my attention to the nettles which were far past their best. As I hadn't dried and stored any from earlier in the year I had to make do with an organic nettle tea bag, (some witch I am!)

I arrived at Sophie's around four in the afternoon feeling rather weary. No food combined with a rather late night finishing off an article which needed to get to the publisher which was finished but then I got a panic and ended up re-writing it at midnight, meant I was quite pooped, a little nauseous and a tad grumpy. Sophie was her shining self however, quite used to the dishevelled appearance of initiates. My grumpiness didn't touch her at all as Sophie had learnt many many moons ago that nothing is personal. I know this because I once asked her what her secret was, how was it that even when things were conspiring against her she remained happy and positive where others like me would have crumbled or at the very least had a good old moan!

"It's all about perspective and choice" she had replied *"and your perspective and choices are dependent upon what you believe. Believe that the world has conspired against you, that you are a poor individual who has been the victim of some injustice and that is what you will be, with all the feelings of despair and anger which will evidence and justify your belief as you descend down into*

your personal pit of hell tying your own hands on your way to the bottom. However, you might instead believe that you are free yet also interconnected to everything else. Nothing has personally happened to you, you are a free agent within a far wider picture and when you believe that, then you realise that where you are is exactly where you have chosen to be no matter how hard or awful it seems at the time. If the situation doesn't change then that's because you haven't changed it. Nothing can manifest for you which is not chosen, if you believe and live that, then you are free because everything is your choice in your life. You may not always be happy but you will certainly be far more content and at peace with yourself and the world".

I find that hard. Sometimes I catch myself thinking Sophie's philosophy of life is just a successful form of denial or even naivety, yet other times, when I stop worrying just for a moment and live from my heart, I feel the wider picture as the boundaries fall away, and in those rare moments of being, I do sense that those boundaries and shackles are of my own making and if I have been so creative as to make such binding limitations then I must be able to unbind them too. Then the feeling of freedom passes as my mind tells me I am deluding myself, although Sophie says it's the mind which is the source of our shackles and blindness. Nonetheless, when I hear on the news of a baby being so abused that their tiny body has suffered excruciating and enduring torture beyond what I can even begin to imagine and that families or whole communities have been wiped out in floods or hurricanes, I just don't understand how such things could have been chosen.

Sophie says that 'chosen' isn't quite the word for it and that an adequate word doesn't seem to exist which can express a reality beyond our current assumptions of cause and effect. The whole perception we have of the world is skewed and as we slowly open our eyes and change, we will find new words which describe our new experiences. I just hope she's right?

Anyway, whether right or not, I felt comfortable and safe in her hands. Sarah arrived about fivish and we sat down in the kitchen to go through my herbs making sure I had not picked anything dangerous or suspect. I was allowed to drink some fruit juice, in fact I was allowed anything I liked, fasting is only a recommendation and although most of us apparently decide to adhere to it, others make gestures and some don't really bother too much. I'm a stickler for getting things right though, I also wanted to get the most out of my experience.

The rest of the tribe sauntered in from six onwards and were all assembled and performing various duties by seven after copious amounts of tea, biscuits and chatting. I did not join in the preparations and instead sat quietly in James' study until I was called. I love the study, it's like an archetypal 'oldyworldy' library from some Hammer Horror film!

The walls are lined with books and there is one of those wheelie staircases which helps you to reach to the top shelves. James is rather more 'popular occult' orientated than Sophie and has various weird and wonderful ornamentations around such as a full size Baphomet and two stuffed crows which he says represent Huginn and Muninn, Odin's familiars but we all rather think he just likes the mysterious quality of stuffed crows! After changing into my robe I relaxed and closed my eyes listening to the chatter and shuffling from beyond the window and after a further hour, as the sounds began to diminish, *Pendragon* came to collect me.

The moon glistened from behind the trees of the sacred space as I followed my guide, and as we entered the familiar tree lined grove I was struck by the quiet and stillness of the scene before me. Usually the tribe are drumming, chanting or both but this time they were sitting quite still in quiet contemplation. Some were crossed legged, hooded, like rocks themselves whilst others were leaning against the great stones breathing deeply and gazing at the moon. None looked at me, none acknowledged my presence.

Cwenhild stood before the crackling fire and beckoned me to her as *Pendragon* took up a meditative pose with the others.

Signalling for me to sit down next to the fire with her *Cwenhild* proceeded to gather a variety of implements, an act to which I felt suddenly afraid as the old memories of strange magical ordeals returned to my mind in ghostly recollection. I was encouraged however, when *Cwenhild* took the herbs which I had collected that morning, cast them into a pestle and mortar and began to grind saying in a slow chant:

"These nine attack against nine venoms, The worm came creeping and tore asunder a man, then Odin took up nine magical rods and smote the serpent, in nine pieces he dispersed. Now these nine herbs have power against the nine magical outcasts, against nine venoms, against nine flying things, against the loathed things that roam the lands." And then repeated *"Ðas nygon ongan wið nygon attrum. Wyrm com snican, toslat he nan, ða genam woden nygan wuldortanas, sloh ða þa næddran þæt heo on nygan tofleah. Nu magon þas nygon wyrta wið nygon wuldorgeflogenum, wið nygon strum ond wið nygon onflygnum, wið malscrunge minra wihta."*

The words were slow, deliberate, delivered in a low intonation with every kneading of the pestle. I could do nothing but watch with captivation as the charm was weaved before me next to the fire amidst trees, stone and moon. My initiation may hardly have even begun yet I was transported in that moment of surprising intimacy with nature.

Cwenhild added oil to the herbal mixture and then something which looked very much like lard or certainly some type of fat or soft wax. All was mixed together carefully and transferred into a small three legged cauldron which sat patiently at the edge of the fire gently warming.

Later on, after the ceremony had finished and the feasting had begun I learned that in ancient times the herbal concoction was brewed into a tea to be drunk during the ritual. Apparently the brew had certain narcotic effects although no one admitted to having tried it. However, today in our anti-drug world where the state has become such a fundamentalist parent that we unconsciously and consciously check and censor our words and actions lest we offend anyone or risk being sued due to a pot hole in our garden path which the post 'person' fell into and twisted their ankle (yes it's happened to me); the tribe simply cannot offer even a mild narcotic experience. Therefore, a different but very powerful alternative has been developed.

Cwenhild placed more logs onto the fire which sprung up in grateful response pouring out more heat and illuminating the circle in the orange glow. I noticed the tribal members still in repose, eyes closed now, drinking in the magical atmosphere growing all around us. All was quiet except for the crackling fire, leaping and jumping with renewed life. *Cwenhild* lifted the portly cauldron from the fire's edge and tested its contents with her finger. With a grunt of satisfaction for a potion well made she leant towards me and whispered *"you must undress Raven so your body may be anointed and cleansed"*.

I have had to undress during an initiation before although this felt so very different. Out in the elements with the earth beneath my feet and the fire warming my skin below the silvery orb of the moon nakedness felt natural, and no one was watching anyway. Years earlier, in the magical order, when I had disrobed the whole lodge were assembled and the men quite literally gawked at my private bits! It always amazed me that every time a young woman was receiving that particular initiation, many men of the lodge would mysteriously decide to attend on that particular day having been absent for some weeks in many cases- I wonder why?

This time I drew the heavy woollen cloak over my head and shoulders before folding it carefully beside me. I added my under clothes and shoes to the small pile whilst instinctively moving closer to the fire for warmth.

Cwenhild gestured for me to stand as she thrust a bundle of dried sage into the flames allowing them to catch. When thick smoke twisted and snaked from the herbs she smudged me, wafting the fragrant bundle up and down then around and around me, cleansing and purifying both my auric and physical bodies. Next she reached for the cauldron. Using a stick with one end wrapped in linen she dubbed the warm concoction from the cauldron and painted the salve onto my pubic bone in front and behind. The same process was afforded the next six chakra points, navel, solar plexus, heart, throat, third eye and crown. Finally, she asked me to turn my hands as they too were anointed with the thick, strange, bitter-sweet smelling salve upon my palms. *"You are anointed and cleansed Raven but that which is stubborn must now be purged. Follow me".*

I was led to the entrance of the sweat lodge where *Cwenhild* knocked on the door three times. A voice emerged from within asking me to enter and I slid into the earthen structure to find *Æthelfrith* sitting crossed legged on the mud floor dressed in a light cotton robe of white. She beckoned me to join her. I sat awkwardly; I was beginning to feel a little nauseous. I think it was the smell of the ointment or perhaps the herbs were penetrating my skin I'm not sure, but I remember feeling a little dazed and sick. *Æthelfrith* took my hands in hers and looked me straight and seriously in the eye. *"What you are about to undertake may change you forever, there is no going back. I must ask you if you wish to continue."* - I think I must have nodded.

Æthelfrith poured a very small amount of water upon the stones releasing a bearable steaming heat. Then she began to chant. I really can't remember what the words were and I have not been given a copy of them but I know they were a summoning of my guides and my totem animal. My eyes were closed and the singing chant and the heat took me into a deep trancelike state. *Æthelfrith* gently put her hands into mine and recited the following ancient spell from the Lacnunga (which I have been given a copy of!):

"*Das nygon ongan wið nygon attrum. Wyrm com snican, toslat he nan, ða genam woden nygon wuldoetanas, sloh ða pa næddran pæt heo on nygoni tofleah, pær geæn dode æppel ond attor, pæt heo næfre ne wolde on hus bugan. Fille ond finule felamihtiga twa, pa wyrte gesceop witig drihtn, halig on heofenum pa he hongode, sette ond sænde on seofon worolde, earmum ond eadigum eallum to bote. Stondeð heo wið wærce, stunað heo wið attre ond seo mæg wið ðrie ond wið triginta, wið feondes hond ond wið heabregde, wið malscrunge minra wihta. Nu magon pas nygon wyrta wið nygon wuldorgeflogenum, wið nygon attrum ond wið nygon onflygnum, wið ðy readan attre, wið ðy runlan attre, wið ðy hwitan attre, wið ðy hæwenan attre, wið ðy geol wan attre, wið ðy grenan attre, wið ðy wonnan attre, wið ðy wedenan attre, wið ðy brunan attre, wið ðy basewan attre, gif ænig attor eactan fleogan, oððe ænig norðan genægan cume, oððe ænig westan ofer werðeode. Oððin stod ofer alde ængancunde: "Ic ana wat ea rinnende ond pa nygon nædran nu behealdað, motan ealle weoda nu wyrtum asringan, sæs toslupan eal sealt wæter, ðonee ic pis attor of ðe geblawe.*"

"These nine spikes against nine poisons. A worm came crawling, he tore a man apart, then Woden took up nine glory-rods, struck the adder then so it flew apart into nine, there apple ended it and its poison so that it would never bend into a house. Chervil and fennel, two of great might, the wise lord shaped these plants while he was hanging, holy in the heavens he set them and sent them into the seven worlds for poor and for wealthy, as a cure for all. It stands against pain, it attacks against poison, it has might against three and thirty, against foeman's hand and against lordly sleight, against bewitching and harmful beings. Now these nine plants have might against nine powerful diseases, against nine poisons and against nine infections, against the red poison, against the running poison, against the white poison, against the pale blue poison, against the yellow poison, against the green poison, against the pale poison, against the dark blue poison, against the bright poison, against the purple poison. If any poison flying from the east or any from the north should come, or any from the west over the tribe of men. Woden stood over the ancient malevolent race: *"I alone know the running rivers and they enclose nine adders, all weeds may now spring up as herbs, seas slide apart, all salt water while I blow this poison from you."*

The last line was repeated again and again as a further chant until I flew up into the air, through the roof of the sweat lodge and high into the sky where I looked down upon the clump of trees surrounding the nine stones. I was Raven. A wolf called from below and I looked down with piercing eyes to see *Æthelfrith* bounding beneath me, sleek and fearsome. I followed her, flying over many fields until the colours began to change and night became day. And our eyes accustomed themselves to the light of the Otherworld. I saw a speck on the horizon which, as we grew nearer became the small grove of trees we had left only moments earlier. This time however, the colours were so vivid and the light so soft I was moved by emotion. As humanity crept back I morphed into me again and I stepped into the sacred place.

I felt a surge of what I can only describe in conflicting terms as a powerful peace wash over and through me. *Æthelfrith,* nuzzled at my hand and as she did so, the ground beneath my feet began to fall away and the grove started to spin becoming a whirl of colour spinning so fast that a tunnel appeared to form with *Æthelfrith* and myself inside. Structure, time, space, everything disappeared in a whir of light and we were pulled or pushed or both through tunnel after tunnel so fast I felt sure that when my feet finally met up with the ground again that I must have left part of myself behind. It seems so stupid to say it was like rushing through wormholes, I've never been through a wormhole but if I had then that is how I imagine it would feel!

Finally I felt terra firma beneath my feet and gaining some

composure I looked about me to see a place so unusually familiar I felt my knees buckle. A house stood before us. A normal looking house in a normal looking street somewhere in Bournemouth, southern England. I say 'somewhere' because when I last saw that house I was four years old and my child's awareness didn't yet stretch to knowing exactly where in Bournemouth we actually lived. I was horrified. I remember looking at *Æthelfrith* with accusing eyes- "why the hell have you brought me here?" She hadn't, I now realise, taken me there at all it was me, all me. I had closed out the worst of that house and the events within it for so many years and had left a part of 'me' behind there, a part of my soul which I was there to retrieve.

Until you have retrieved a part of your soul it is impossible to really comprehend what it means. I had always been rather dubious of the whole idea, wasn't the soul essentially whole? How on earth could something like the soul ever be fragmented? I now understand though, how our soul really can become fragmented by severe trauma.

The soul is linked to our consciousness which in this reality contains and relates to our earthly situations and our emotional reactions to them. It is different to our spirit which always remains whole and distanced from this incarnate reality although the spirit always retains an energetic link which some powerful shamans can use to travel to the upper worlds which are apparently so beautiful, some choose not to return.

It is impossible however, for the consciousness to unite with spirit and travel to such great heights if the soul is fragmented. We need to bring back all the parts we have left behind, the parts which are still holding onto the traumas, disappointments and pain, the parts which call to us silently, pleading for comfort and nourishment, parts which we ignore or even worse, project onto others, so fearful are we to welcome them back. I was fearful standing there before that house again. I felt a tightness in my chest and tears welled up in my eyes as the scene unfolded before me.

It was twilight and *Æthelfrith,* now in human form too, took my hand and guided me towards the side of the house where we could hear a commotion occurring inside. We managed to gain a view of what was going on by peering in through the dining room window. There were four people sitting round a normal family table two adults, man and woman and two children both girls. A golden Labrador called Sandy was lying on the rug by the door which led into a long hallway.

It was an idyllic scene until sound was added which made sense of the woman's contorted face. She was shouting at the small girl to her right who didn't seem to want to eat any food. My awareness began to drift. I moved between the small child and myself as vision and memory began to sync. I felt the little girl's terror. No I didn't want to eat, I was too terrified to eat without vomiting. Every moment in that house was a hell that I had never wanted to return to. Food was the focus of it all at first until the violence of her vindictive side became so normal for the woman that anything would set her off.

I had gone to that family to be cared for. They were fostering me after I had been taken away from my Mother who was a chronic alcoholic. The new family were lovely at first but it was all so very strange, especially the food. I didn't recognise it, I had always had chips and beans, not lettuce, tomatoes and spinach. It was all too much too soon and this woman hated that I found it difficult to eat her food and so hated me too. I would often be sick from the anxiety of it all. When I couldn't eat, first due to the strangeness and then due to the terror which rendered me in a semi-catatonic state she would turn on me.

Watching from the window I saw the child which was me being pulled from her chair, too scared even to cry out she was dragged across the dining room floor, the other child, the natural daughter was looking on quite accustomed by now to her mother's violent behaviour towards me. The mother took my little hands in hers and as she entered the hallway began beating me up and down against the floor in just the same way I beat out the rugs at home. Up and down I beat them against the ground outside, dust flying everywhere making me cough. I had never seen a child being beaten in the same way. Dust did not fly from me however, it was vomit and then the warmth of yellow urine.

Unable to stand the repetitive beating, up and down against the floor my stomach had heaved and my bladder had released, just as it had done every time she hit and beat me. As she dragged me to the kitchen I knew what was happening even though I couldn't see, as memory and awareness returned to me with full force. I crumpled by that window in agonising deep sobs as I saw in my mind how the mother poured boiling water from the kettle into the washing up bowl where a cloth floated around the bottom, put the bowl on the floor next to me and instructed me to grab the cloth and clean up the mess. The boiling water was impossible to bear and she laughed at my attempts to grab the cloth from the scalding water. Next, searching for more satisfaction she took a tea spoon out of a drawer, put it in my hand and sneered *"well if you won't clean up the mess you can eat it up then!"*

Perhaps deciding that eating vomit may just produce more she suddenly yanked my right arm pulling me from the floor, opened the side door and threw me outside. I fell hard onto the concrete step gashing my arm. And then we saw each other. I was crumpled on the ground yards from the step where I sat in my nightdress, rocking back and forth not knowing what else to do but just wait for my carers to let me in again.

I looked at that small, vulnerable shape, too scared to say a word and went and took her hand. She looked bewildered, like a kitten I once saw on the news being kicked by a girl too drunk to know what she was doing. The mother wasn't drunk however and I wonder to this day what has become of her daughter who witnessed such abuse and at times was even encouraged to view me as an animal which could be hit and kicked. It was then I saw the neighbour, staring out of her kitchen. I had heard some years later you see that there had been a report to the social services that I had been seen sitting on the back door step in my nightdress in the dark and the cold.

I sent a thankful blessing to that neighbour who may very well have saved my life and I took the cold bleeding child in my arms. I knew what was due to happen. The husband would argue with the mother to let me back in and I would be put to bed. The next morning she would find the gash on my arm and ask me "how did that get there?" I would answer that it happened when she threw me out of the house and she would drop my arm with a grunt and storm out. Not this time though! Looking my younger self in the eyes I told her *"it's time to come home, if you want to. I want you to come home"* and she clung to me like a scared animal and we walked away from that house towards the silver grey wolf now waiting on the lamp lit pavement.

Paws turning we followed our guide. Time was faster now and before even one thought had opportunity to make itself known I was back in the earthen womb of the sweat lodge. My body felt fluid, skin slipping, hair like feathers. Water met with hot stone filling my head with steam. Every pour opened and flowed with sweet long stored liquids. A wolf said *"now you are ready to release all the negativity to the heat. Come out when you are ready and call for help if you need it, we will check on you often."* With a blast of icy air, a wolf disappeared through a small door.

Apparently I remained in the sweat lodge for a further hour or so. Reality swam and my ability to recollect what occurred is limited. Having retrieved my largest piece of missing soul my being was able to purge a large quantity of negative and repressing energy which had taken its place for almost twenty years. Later, Sophie told me that sometimes, a person may not be quite ready to re-absorb the lost part of their soul and all the memories that it brings. In such situations the soul is still retrieved but the healing takes place over a longer period of time with the person's guides parenting the soul piece until the uniting can occur. Despite the memories and the re-lived trauma, I had been ready. The past year had prepared me for the event and although there were certainly other parts of my soul still waiting for me this has been the greatest step of all.

I was exhausted when finally I re-emerged from the lodge where I was washed down with cold water. I stood before *Æthelfrith* whilst four tribe members came forward carrying goblets of blessed water from the elemental quarters. *Æthelfrith* dipped the forefinger of her right hand into the first goblet from the east and traced a pentacle over my heart chakra saying *"May you be blessed and purified and encouraged in fearlessness and serenity"*, dipping again in the goblet from the south she traced the pentacle upon my throat chakra saying *"may you speak wisdom in all things"*. *Æthelfrith* continued by anointing my solar plexus with water from the west- *"may you have clarity and control of passions through the art of serene discrimination"* and finally, from the goblet of the north, all my seven chakra points and the two on my hands were anointed similarly- *"may your wisdom combine with action in security and true knowledge."* I was then instructed to kneel and *Æthelfrith,* standing over me, blew on the top of my head with some force, empowering me.

Initiations or rites of passage as we prefer to call them are not what is normally understood by the term 'initiation' in most modern magical groups. For the wicce it was never about the revelation of secret knowledge or hidden arcane mysteries. Initiation meant and does mean to us, the movement and enabling of energy to encourage the development of the traveller to become their own centre of revelation. The group does not hold the secrets like some powerful, tantalising, ego alluring entity; the group is an energy conduit. Some rites prepare for energy movement, others release blocks to the flowing whilst others increase the vibrational frequency of our energy. The first rite is exoteric, the second esoteric and the third, which I may never experience, is mystic. Beyond that are three further rites building on the mystic path which few ever reach in this lifetime.

We ate a hearty feast although I did not take any wine which would have gone straight to my head. Feeling a little more human but terribly tired I made the short journey home, falling into my bed at what must have been about 1.00 a.m where I did something I never usually do. I fell straight to sleep. My nightly rituals of checking the doors are locked, checking the plug points are off and worrying about the following day were absent and I slept deeper than I have ever slept before. What can I now say? What words are there to describe? I wish we had the words and I hope one day we shall but for now all I can offer is this:

'I had allowed my own demons to possess me for too long, welcoming them as guardians of my heart and soul. They had convinced me that no heart could fill with such pain without breaking and no mind could hold such memories without destroying itself and so the demons held me strong. But now I have searched and faced the demon's fears so the pain and the anguish, disappeared into the love I felt for that crumpled little girl sitting in her nightdress on the concrete step. She is home'.

Souling Day (an evening of tuition)

I visited Sophie tonight to receive the first instruction of my new degree as each of us has ongoing guidance and tuition in the weeks following our rites of passage. It's a time where the *ealdor* mentoring us can teach new meditations and exercises and assess where we are and if we are having any difficulties or have any concerns. I arrived about sixish and James made himself scarce as Sophie and I took over the kitchen. We had become good friends and after our meetings I would often stay for supper so we had settled into a now familiar routine. Sophie and I prepare the food together, tonight we had slow cooked lamb with jacket potatoes and salad, then, whilst it's cooking we go to the living room, light incense and candles and begin with a short breathing mediation in order to leave the stresses and strains of the day to one side and focus ourselves on the task in hand.

Tonight Sophie taught me a new daily routine which I am to adopt for as long and consistently as possible. It is composed of four meditational exercises performed at four times of the day. When I awake I am to sit quietly for a while, it need not be too long, even five minutes will suffice and contemplate how the relationship between our material world and the Otherworld interacts causally and how this causal relationship emerged from nothingness. At midday or close to it I am to take some time to meditate more fully by repeating in my head the following mantra:

"My body is as the mountain.
My eyes are as the oceans.
My mind is as the sky."

At sunset I am to mediate again combining a breathing exercise with a mantra which again focuses upon the apparent dichotomy between everything which exists and manifests and that which does not. When breathing in I am to contemplate that which exists like saying on the in-breath something like *"knowledge is manifest, therefore it exists"* followed by the out breath and- *"Knowledge does not exist, it returns to nothingness."* Just before bed I must hold in my mind the image of a lotus flower with five petals coloured white, red, blue, green and yellow respectively being held in my heart chakra whilst at the same time holding a pure white lotus flower above my head, all in my imagination of course. There is a further development to this final stage which Sophie will tell me at our next instruction. This meditative process is apparently based upon an ancient practice first recorded in Tibet and it is designed to awaken and expand consciousness from the limited to the unlimited and back to the limited once more but in renewed form. This, as Sophie patiently explained, is the process of lasting magical transformation.

P

6. FINAL

Wyrd bið ful āræd

(Fate is inexorable)

It would be considered quite usual and even expected for this, the concluding chapter, to reflect upon the journey so far and perhaps to consider where such a journey may take us in the future. Yet in a world where up may well be down and reality illusion, perhaps the usual summaries, reflections and postulations should be put to one side, at least for the moment whilst we give voice to the unusual. Let us, at this ending point, return to the beginning which although giving birth to the journey has only been glimpsed within the narrative, waiting patiently for the journey's end when author and reader have readied themselves for its wisdoms. It is not a new story, and we have touched upon it earlier but I hope that its deeper, more transcendental qualities may now shine through the words just as our imagination, magic and poetry have now flourished and balanced with logic, analysis and evaluation. Let us begin.

Three sisters sit beneath the World Ash Tree called *Yggdrasil:*

Ask veit eg standa, heitir Yggdrasill, hár baðmur, ausinn hvíta auri; þaðan koma döggvar þær er í dala falla, stendur æ yfir grænn Urðarbrunni.

(An ash I know stands, its name is Yggdrasil, An immense tree, covered over by the white sand. Thence come the dew that falls in the valleys, it stands ever-green above the well of Urdal).

The great spring of creation, Urdal, flows freely from the first spark of divine being. Urdal never runs dry as it nourishes the tree of life upon which, all our Gods and we humans depend. This sacred space is guarded by the three sisters who weave the firmaments of all creation from potential, into form and matter, bringing into unjudged fruition both dreams and nightmares.

The sister's names are *Wyrd* (that which has become), *Vernandi* (that which is being) and *Skuld* (that which will become). They stand therefore, for the very pre-conditions of our consciousness as they weave past, present and future from one source or as the bravest of physicists might say, one singularity. Some of the threads they weave are subtle, others seem conflicting and it is from this first source, the beginning of all, we may now consider in more detail some of the deeper mysteries of an ancient magical consciousness, and wonder at how far we could truly embrace them today.

Free-will versus fate

If *Wyrd* is indeed *bið ful áræd* then one could be forgiven for wondering why on earth we worry about doing anything or changing anything at all. If we are simply the puppets of fate then what is the point of it all, and what is the point of magic if really, nothing can ever be altered? However, from the flavour of the journey taken so far into the ancient shamanic past of the wicce, we may begin to sense that our concept of 'free-will' is very different from the notion of 'being free'. Free will is something we think we have or should have whereas 'freedom' is a state of being. Freedom is not an object, physical or otherwise which we may 'have' or can obtain or can exercise in our lives. Freedom is not a 'thing'. The implications of what this means are difficult to grasp because when we think about anything at all we are immediately conceptualising the content of the thought as an object, something external to us in some way, which then requires transferring into the subject of our thoughts. We make everything a 'thing' and lose 'it' in the process!

Let us look at the web therefore, in a different way. Imagine the three sisters sitting at the base of the great tree weaving their web of destiny which creates every moment, moving from limitless to limited realities, fool to magician to high priestess and beyond.

Our contemporary assumption of this primordial creative energy which flows unbounded, is that it must be an ultimate form of power, the pinnacle of the hierarchy, and as everything emanates from this ultimate source it must be our life's goal to return to that source as our final destination. We wrongly assume albeit implicitly, that there is an end in sight to this journey of lives where we will once again reach or return to nirvana. It rarely occurs to us however, that this energetic movement of divine creation is a two way reciprocal affair and that the web of destiny is not a determining phenomenon flowing towards an end goal, it is fluid, free and eternal. There is no final destination; there is only movement and vibration reaching to infinity and the magical journeying is our expression of this movement. The end is a constant revealing of now.

Thinking of the web in this way illuminates reality as a realm not of objects to be conceptualised, but as a realm of constant potential. Every moment is potential and the actualisation or manifestation of that moment as a physical or mental occurrence, is immediately in the past. Whenever we have a thought about something be it a physical, mental, emotional or even spiritual the 'object' of our thought and the thought considering it, is left behind us as a new potential enters and becomes the present. It is our perception alone which creates our constructs of time, and as we believe that perception requires us to objectify everything we are aware of and not aware of; we live always and consistently in the immediate past.

We sense a determining principle to fate and thus a diminishing of freedom, because our perception is always focused on this immediate past which apparently cannot be changed, and thus we mistake this past for the present. The present of constant ever flowing potential is lost to us in our misguided beliefs of what constitutes perception and it the imagination which must be brought forward to distinguish the manifest past, from the potentialised and free present, until we can do this, we only ever see illusions and shadows. If we can achieve this state of living at least occasionally within the potential of the present, we can begin to fully experience how the imagination is 'world creating'. We create, or can create our world in every moment. No domination or will-power is required, just an immersion into the freedom of being in each potential moment, the state of both the Tarot's Fool and paradoxically, the World.

In this way we move from the fool to the magician to the high priestess, and then the formed archetypal manifestations which continue into the familiar realms. The fool is potentialised energy, pure, trusting, knowing nothing and everything equally. The magician stands, right hand to the spiritual realm and the left hand directing this Otherworldly energy to the manifest earth, never willing or demanding, simply immersing within the flow and enabling what already is, to where it already needs to go, guided by the wisdom of the high priestess. Then form explodes from the void, whirling into high concentrations of dense energy where a painful dichotomy appears to occur between the divine beauty of that first moment of our being, and the tangible earthiness of our embodied humanity. Ego then attempts to bridge the unbridgeable, commenting to us within a stream of internal dialogue which we mistake for reality as it whispers to us of a divine homeland, now lost but reachable if only we continue to listen to its ramblings. Yet these ramblings, just as thoughts, are in the past and of the past, whereas communing with the energy in perfect trust is the action of the ever present magical world. This often appears as paradoxical yet all a paradox does is to indicate a level of understanding which is not yet revealed.

Such ponderings are now entering the conceptual realms of transcendental metaphysics and for any who would like to explore this aspect of enquiry further, may I recommend the great existential philosophers and their contemporaries. It is not my intention however, to present a philosophical thesis here, as so many philosophers have laboured and toiled at the edges of their consciousness in search of such a goal and one wonders, occasionally, at what has actually been achieved by doing so. One would do far better to read Yeats and listen to Beethoven, as it is in the poetic and creative experience that magic still flows unhindered. My focus remains on the shamanic origins of modern witchcraft which can be traced through the writings, traditions and experiences of the Anglo-Saxon wicce to revitalise the modern Craft, and re-enchant our contemporary world.

I often wonder what Gerald Gardner would have made of the figure of the ancient wicce, the Anglo-Saxon witch had he been writing today. During the 1950's, dark ages England appeared to be relatively unknown with only Godfrid Storm's 'Anglo-Saxon Magic' reaching any book stores at all. We can therefore, forgive Gardner for believing that with regard to witchcraft *'there is no trace of Saxon customs in the cult [witchcraft], it does not seem that such Saxon witches as there were ever came into it.'* Perhaps he did not have access to the magical Anglo-Saxon manuscripts available to us today from The British Library.

Had Gardner benefitted from such access, I believe his research would have been even more extensive and rich, and small inconsistencies which we find in his writings would have been corrected. For example, I have no doubt he would have realised that the mysterious words he refers to as being evidence of an ancient and secret language of the witches, words such as halch, dwale and ganch, are in fact Anglo-Saxon words (halch for example meant a meadowland in the Scottish Boarders but more widely within England it meant to hug or embrace), as is of course, the word Wicca.

Yet in the 1950's the dark ages of Anglo-Saxon England were believed lost to us, and Gardner could not have benefited from the sources we have at our fingertips today. More than this, the dark ages were thought to be a time which was better lost lest we have cause to remember and 'own' the apparently barbaric, confused and pitiful era which to many marks the worst point of uncivilised ancestry we have in this land. With our romanticised fictions of the earlier Celts and Britons with their tales of heroic Kings and wise wizards, the Anglo-Saxons have always seemed to be a rather different kettle of fish. Fighting, whoring and pillaging contrast strikingly with the wisdom of Merlin, the heroism of knights and the beauty of mysterious Princesses. 'Anglo-Saxon' remains for many of us, a dirty word.

Furthermore, and this can only be speculative, Gardner may have known perfectly well that witchcraft has Anglo-Saxon origins, after all Tolkien's work, published only a few years before Gardner's draws heavily upon this *Middengeard,* so sources could not have been completely lacking for a researcher such as Gardner. Yet following the Second World War, I doubt Gardner would have wished an Anglo-Saxon and thus Germanic association to his resurrection of the Craft.

But let us now be clear. Wicca is an Anglo-Saxon word describing an ancient tradition of witchcraft exposed by the great

Gerald Gardner. It is shamanic in origin, stretching from far pre-history where we see figures dancing in circles upon walls of caves, shapeshifting into animal spirits who guide them in their magical journeying, through to more religio-social groups who worship the trinitarian Goddess in greenwood shrines by sacred springs, and others who now worship the God with his nailed son, within the walls and edifices of stone churches. All of us who move energy are using magic and those who have skill and insight enough immerse into its deep waters and re-emerge empowered to direct change within the world, are witches. There is no one 'real' type of witchcraft, only one source experienced and utilised in a myriad of different ways.

Weaving the past and future

Let us not fear the wyrd sisters, maiden, hag and crone. After all, we witches are weaving with them. This is the truth of the two way energy flow. If we immerse within the energy of the Otherworld as the wicce have taught, then we become the sisters of past, present and future creating our own web out of many colourful threads, weaving each intricate design with our spell song.

The most richly coloured tapestries are those woven with love and awareness of being. Tapestries such as these affect all those who look upon them, inspiring and healing others through strength of beauty. So many tapestries are woven limply however, with the few colours ignorance and fear provide. The threads are sparse and vulnerable to disarray, being blown to and fro with the whims of the wind never finding that inner security, peace and joy which blossoms from a web well woven. So finally we have come to the one foundational choice which so many great teachers have attempted time and again to offer humanity, do we wish to weave in awareness or ignorance? Can we bear to recognise who we truly are, the creators of manifestations?

It has been my aim within these pages to expand upon this remarkably simple yet profoundly difficult choice by presenting an exploration of the origins of witchcraft in England, to inspire all those of us who retain a spiritual or genetic heritage to this small yet enigmatic island nestling at the edge of Europe and Scandinavia. If the principles and wisdom's of the ancient wicce can be incorporated more fully into today's Craft workings and life in general, then we can change our current world by 'dreaming a new dream' as the shamans say. If we can understand that the sisters of the World Ash Tree do not determine the past, present and future as is commonly supposed, but rather, reveal what we choose to actualise and manifest, then we can evolve our relationship with witchcraft and life further still.

As the energy of their web is two way, and everything effects and is interconnected to everything else, then what we choose to manifest as our present causes reciprocal ripples along each fibre of the web within which we are weaved, and these ripples change the past as well as the future. This is an extremely counter-intuitive concept. How can the past be changed? How can a memory which has been with me for life ever become something which it is not, how is this possible? It is possible because memory is not the past, it is but a reflection and a poor one at that, of an event which we choose to bind ourselves to. A memory is not 'real' it is an attachment to a story which we use over and over again to construct our worlds. Our memory of the past is not the past, it is simply the tale (*sēo talu*) we tell ourselves.

There is therefore, an even greater magic at work, a magic which the wicce with their subtle yet profound cosmology understood. If we make a change today it alters not just the future, but the past as well. This means that a healing made a sustained today, whether it be a healing of a genetic predisposition, or a behaviour or a psychological trait which has been 'nurtured' for generations, then that healing begins a process of transformation which

160

ripples back and forwards, altering our own experience of life, our children's experience of life and also, the experiences of our ancestors. And, as the healing continues into future generations, more of the positive energy created by the change will ripple back throughout the web, until the whole ancestral line reverberates with the effects within their own lives which are happening right now, outside of time as we know it.

In a world saturated with every type of therapeutic intervention you can possibly imagine, healing at its most fundamental level still reduces to two energetic principles, belief and choice. Unfortunately for us, we tend to believe in pain and choose the resultant fear, and sadly we teach our children similarly. How can we even begin to teach our children that imagination is *'a powerful creative faculty*, [with] *a capacity to reform nature"* (Kneller, p.52) if we don't truly believe it ourselves? The great philosopher Immanuel Kant even stated that the imagination can create a world *'that surpasses nature'*. What wonders are within our reach therefore, what beauty and majesty lay just beyond the tips of our fingers waiting for us to open our eyes?

This book has started a process which I hope continues to ripple far beyond its pages. It is an answer to a heartfelt call for meaning and truth beyond the material world of things and social obligation. It reminds us that witches are part of an ancient heritage weaved within the very land that throbs beneath our feet, stretching back in time. If we can listen intently, observe closely and experience fully this call for a more bountiful relationship with our great Mother, then we will bring about a healing so powerful and permanent, it will re-enchant our world for everyone. But this is not a passive calling. Few people manage to move convincingly beyond ignorance as to do so requires a struggle and searching rarely supported within the parameters permitted or enabled within our society. Yet if we can journey to the magical Otherworld with the tool of imagination, swimming from the limited to the unlimited and back again, every time we return we do so with magic and wonder which raises and expands the energy of this mortal reality that little bit higher and wider. Furthermore, by bringing this magic into being we achieve the great alchemical prize, we make what is unknown known and that my dear sisters and brothers, is the path to enlightenment on all levels.

APPENDIX

A guide to Old English (OE) pronunciation

Old English was and still is, a language which conjures energy and power. If you have access to a computer I would recommend going onto YouTube, putting in the words 'Beowulf Old English' and listening to OE speakers reciting the introductory verses to this ancient epic poem. A particularly evocative reading can be found at: http://www.youtube.com/watch?v=4LVTH8ii_8. Even better, learn to read it yourself and then add to the recitation a roaring fire, strong ale and good company to create a magical evening.

I present here a basic guide to OE pronunciation giving the Modern English (ME) sounds to the OE letters. The guide does assume the speaker to have a British, Received English accent (like the 'BBC' or 'Queen's English'). I apologise to all those who do not have such an accent but I hope Received English is common enough to provide all readers with some idea of the required sounds.

By the conclusion of this guide you should be able to say the title of this book correctly, read out loud the opening of Beowulf and have the basics necessary to tackle the charms within this book.

Vowels

There are short and long vowels in OE, just as we have today. For example, consider the two words 'sat' and 'sad'. The first has a short 'a' sound and the second, a longer more drawn out sound. We instinctively 'know' which sound to use but for those not familiar with our language, knowing when to use a long or short vowel sound can be very confusing. OE can be equally challenging. Some scribes did use an acute accent over certain letters to distinguish short from long vowels but they were very inconsistent in the practice. Later scholars have been helpful however, and include macrons, short dashes above letters to identify long vowels. For example, the OE word 'Hwæt' (generally meaning a call to attention such as What! Listen! or Lo!) is pronounced 'Hwat' with a short 'a' like 'sat'. The word 'hwǣr' (where), is pronounced 'hwar' with the 'a' as in 'sad' and this difference is indicated by the macron. Below is a list of vowels and their sounds.

OE   ME

Short vowels

a	as in	'but'
æ		'sat'
e		'set'
i		'tin'
o		'body'
u		'pull'
y	sounded as the 'ou' in 'you'	

Long vowels

ā	as in	'hard'
ǣ		'sad'
ē		'jade'
ī		'bead'
ō		'hoard'
ū		'booed'
ý	as in the French	'sur'

Consonants

b d l m n p r t w   are generally sounded as in ME.

cw   is sounded as our modern 'q'

sc   is sounded 'sh'

cc   is sounded 'ch'

cg   is sounded 'dge' so the OE word 'brycg' (bridge) sounds very similar to the ME, 'bridge'.

When *c* is next to an *e* or *i* it becomes 'ch', so the OE word 'cild' (child) is also pronounced similarly to the word child today. When a *c* appears at the beginning of a word however, it tends to be pronounced as a k sound, so 'cætt' sounds as 'cat'.

An *f* becomes like a *v* in the middle of a word so 'heofan' (heaven) is again very similar to its ME equivalent, heaven. Similarly, an *s* in the middle of a word often sounds like a *z*, so 'freosan' sounds quite like its modern form, 'freeze'. A notable difference in OE however, is that almost every letter is sounded out, unlike today, where many letters especially at the ends of words have become silent. So if in doubt, say it out! The word 'wiccecræft' should now be well within your grasp, just remember to sound out the *e* in the middle.

New letters

Two letters not found at all in ME are:

ð and *þ* which are both sounded as in the 'th' in the girls name 'Beth'. With macrons, and at the beginning of words they become slightly more forceful, more akin to the 'th' in the word 'the'.

Diphthongs

Diphthongs are two vowels which glide into each other within the space of one syllable. There are two main diphthongs in OE. They are *ea* and *eo*. The first letter elongates with the second being slightly less important. For example, *ea* is still in use today in the words bear and wear. The pronunciation is almost the same too although as Stephen Pollington points out, in OE, it is perhaps closer in sound to the *ai* in the surname 'Baird'.

Practice

Here are the first few lines of Beowolf (Prologue):

Hwæt wē Gār- Dena in geār-dagum
Þēod-cyninga þrym gefrūnon,
Hū ðā æþelingas Ellen fremedon.
Oft Scyld Scēfing sceaþena þrēatum,
Monegum mægþum meodo-setla oftēah;
Egsode Eorl, syððan ærest wearð
Fēasceaft funden; hē þæs frōfre gebād:
Wēox under wolcnum, weorð-myndum þāh,
Oðþæt him æghwylc þāra ymb-sittendra
Ofer hron-rāde hæran scolde,
Gomban gyldan: þæt wæs gōd cyning!

Lo!, praise of the prowess of people-kings
of spear-armed Danes, in days gone by,
we have heard, and what honour the athelings won!
Often Scyld the Scefing from squadroned foes,
from many a tribe, the mead-bench tore,
awing the earls. Since erst he lay
friendless, a foundling, fate repaid him:
for he waxed under welkin, in wealth he throve,
till before him the folk, both far and near,
who house by the whale-path, heard his mandate,
gave him tributes: that was a good King!

   Listen to the prologue on the internet and then have a go at saying it along with the reader, it really isn't as hard as it may look. Also, you may begin to hear that although some words look very different to ME they actually sound almost the same. In the last line we see the word 'þæt' (that) which is pronounced as 'that', so it looks strange but sounds quite normal! You may have noticed however, that within the charms from the magical manuscripts, no macrons appear to guide our pronunciation. The scribes were just not that helpful! Their intention was to transcribe and collect together a treatise of medical remedies which although surviving from a far earlier oral tradition, were not necessarily going to be read aloud ever again. Therefore, just like today, you simply have to 'know' when to use a long or short vowel sound and this comes with time and practice. However, as a very general rule, long vowels appear at the beginning of words as in 'toothpaste' and 'bearded' rather than 'bizarre'.

For a more in-depth study of OE I would recommend 'First steps in Old English' by Stephen Pollington which includes a short dictionary with macrons. Also, 'Complete Old English (Anglo-Saxon)' by Mark Atherton, which includes an extremely useful CD.

BIBLIOGRAPHY:

Avens, R. (1980) *'Imagination is Reality'*, Spring Publications Inc, Putnam, Connecticut.

Avila, T. (1987 2nd edition) *'The collected works of St. Teresa of Avila Volume One'*, Translated by Kavanaugh, K. And Rodriguz, O. ICS Publications, Washington, D.C.

Bates, B. (2002) *'The Real Middle Earth: Magic and Mystery in the Dark Ages'*, Pan Books.

Bates, B. (1996) *'The Wisdom Of The Wyrd: Teachings for today from our ancient past '*, Rider.

Cheetham, T. (2003) *'The World Turned Inside Out: Henry Corbin and Islamic Mysticism'*, Spring Journal Books, Woodstock, Connecticut.

David-Neel, A. (1931) *'Initiations and Initiates in Tibet'*, Rider and Company LTD.

Fabing, H. (1956) *'On Going Berserk: A Neurochemical Inquiry.'* Scientific Monthly. 83 [Nov. 1956]

Gardner, G. (1959) *'The Meaning of Witchcraft'*, Weisser Books,

Bibliography

Boston, 2004.

Greene, R. (2000) *'The Magic of Shapeshifting'*, Weiser Books, Boston.

Greenwood, S. (2005) *'The Nature of Magic: An Anthropology of Consciousness'*, Berg, Oxford, New York.

Greenwood, S. (2009) *'The Anthropology of Magic'*, Berg, Oxford, New York.

Greenwood, S. (2000) *'Magic, Witchcraft And The Otherworld'*, Berg, Oxford, New York.

Hartmann, T. (1998) *'The Last Hours of Ancient Sunlight'*, Hodder and Stoughton.

Heidegger, M. (1927) *'Being and Time'* second edition, Mulhall, S. (ed), Routledge, 2005.

Kieckhefer, R. (2000) *'Magic in the Middle Ages'* Cambridge University Press.

Kneller, J. (2007) *'Kant and the Power of Imagination'*, Cambridge Univeristy Press.

Linsell, T. (1994) *'Anglo-Saxon Mythology, Migration and Magic'*, Anglo-Saxon Books.

Perkins, J. (1997) *'Shape Shifting: Techniques for Global and Personal Transformation'*, Destiny Books, Vermont.

Perkins, J. (1994) *'The World is as You Dream It'*, Destiny Books, Vermont.

Piers, V. (1995) *'Shamanism'*, University of Oklahoma Press.

Plato Complete Works, Cooper, J.M. (ed), (1997), Hackett Publishing Company Ltd.

Pollington, S. (2000) *'Leechcraft, Early English Charms, Plantlore and Healing'*, Anglo-Saxon Books.

169

Raff, J. (2000) *'Jung and the Alchemical Imagination'* Nicolas-Hays, Inc, Berwick, Maine.

Rosales, O. (2009) *'Elemental Shaman'*, Llewellyn Publications, Woodbury, Minessota.

Schlutz, A. (2009) *'Mind's World'*, University of Washington Press, Seattle and London.

Von Franz, M.L. (1979) *'alchemical active imagination'*, Shambhala, Boston and London.

Voss, A. (1992) *'Magic, Astrology and Music: The background to Marsillio Ficino's astrological music therapy and his role as a renaissance magus'*, unpublished work.

The Anglo-Saxon magical manuscripts are stored in The British Library and are known as the Harley 585 collection, and Royal M.S 12. D. xvii.

Lightning Source UK Ltd.
Milton Keynes UK
01 January 2010

165098UK00001B/83/P

9 780956 188625